DANIÈLE BOTT

CHANEL

COLLECTIONS AND CREATIONS

with 159 illustrations, 101 in colour

Thames & Hudson

First published in the United Kingdom in 2007 by
Thames & Hudson Ltd, 181A High Holborn, London WC1V 7QX

www.thamesandhudson.com

First published in 2007 in hardcover in the United States of America by
Thames & Hudson Inc., 500 Fifth Avenue, New York, New York 10110

thamesandhudsonusa.com

This 2007 edition published by Thames & Hudson Ltd
by arrangement with Edigroup-Ramsay.

British Library Cataloguing-in-Publication Data
A catalogue record for this book is available from the British Library

Library of Congress Catalog Card Number 2007900609

ISBN   978-0-500-51360-6

Printed and bound in China

CONTENTS

INTRODUCTION

A land of secrets, dreams and fantasies; a sanctuary protected from the ravages of memory – this is the place where the Chanel legacy is preserved. It was a privilege to discover these original designs, the heart of a fabulous house that has never stopped beating, still pulsing to the rhythm of the future. These early masterpieces are keystones of the Chanel style – a style that can only be defined as a gift, a taste for modernity. We have tried to understand this style, and to capture its quintessential characteristics. Describing the genesis of these creations then allows us to analyse the more recent designs that are their direct descendants.

Follow the thread of time back almost a hundred years, to the period between 1912 and 1919, when a young Gabrielle Chanel was creating her first hats, then her radically simple fashions, which went on to enchant Paris. It is at this point, at the dawn of the age of Chanel, that we find the basis of a dazzling present and of an even more resplendent future. This nostalgia-free museum – the preferred term is *conservatoire* – houses some exceptional pieces, visible clues, sublime and authentic creations by one of the greatest designers of the century. Coco Chanel would have disliked the term *couturière*, literally 'dressmaker', with which she has sometimes been saddled: 'I don't know how to sew', she would have responded with her characteristic wit, bluntness and husky voice. But fashion – Couture with a capital C – became an indissoluble part of her life, and her ultimate destiny. Chanel wove a new world of fashion and sculpted a timeless silhouette. With determination, a visionary instinct, an extraordinary talent for life and an innate sense of elegance, she invented the modern woman.

The magic, the miracle of Chanel – now an empire as famous and as secretive as its founder – is echoed in the strong link between past and present. The connection between an original design and its modern interpretation is a fascinating one. These 'relics' of elegance have lost none of their seductive

Above
Coco Chanel before 1914. An exquisitely delicate profile, with thick dark hair that she herself cut short on a whim a few years later.

Opposite
The Chanel look, a modern woman of adventure as seen and drawn by Karl Lagerfeld.

appeal today, because they show how a style was born. When displayed next to their modern-day incarnations, they still seem utterly contemporary.

In the Chanel archives, the evening gowns created by Mademoiselle sparkle like a million stars, the soft tweed jackets boast exquisite gilt buttons recalling the fashion queen's favourite signs and symbols. Here, in the *conservatoire*, hidden away from indiscreet eyes, time seems to stand still, as if shielded by a screen of subtle luxury: pearls glow, diamonds glitter, baroque stones shine with deep, intense and provocative colours; chains twist around interlocking Cs – the signature monogram created in 1921. Black boxes open to reveal a myriad of camellias, the iconic flower that is a lasting trademark of the couture house on the rue Cambon. Beauty products displayed in their little cases of shining black – the anti-colour she skilfully placed at centre stage from the very beginning – recall a ritual, a silhouette. The image of a visionary artist: Coco Chanel.

The very name of Chanel defies all concepts of time. The house of Chanel has dressed a century and lasted a century, and kindly agreed to satisfy our curiosity and help us to interpret the house icons and symbols. We wanted to decipher this 'grammar' – as Karl Lagerfeld calls it – that lies at the root of the Chanel myth in order to reveal its fundamental features.

The pages of this book are studded with images, photographs and drawings that create a bridge between an often distant past and a prodigious present. There is a constant shifting dialogue, from a black dress of the twenties to a braided suit of the fifties, from a simple lipstick to an eyeshadow compact, right up to contemporary creations which often replicate to the letter the key elements of exquisite sophistication. This allows us to see clever subversions, unexpected interpretations, shifts from one world to another. Every theme, symbol, design and object is evidence of a singular enduring vision.

Mademoiselle owned twenty-one Coromandel screens. Baroque or classic, what counted the most for Coco Chanel was style. Her own unique style was the most copied in the world. Photo Boris Lipnitzki, 1937.

We see the fashion, the world, the galaxy, the signs and symbols that Coco Chanel first created back in the twenties, and gain a better understanding of her extraordinary creativity, and we are also dazzled to discover the amazing skill and talent of those who stand at the helm of Chanel today. Their objectives are the perpetuation of the Chanel image and brand above all, but also the exaltation of elegance, luxury, audacity and daring.

Through five chapters, each based on one of Chanel's five iconic symbols – our way of paying homage to Chanel N° 5, Mademoiselle's fragrance and lucky number – we follow the thread of modernity with constant references to those whose magic touch and creative skill have created such a dynamic company and such lasting style. Jacques Helleu, guardian of the temple, artistic director and architect of the timeless Chanel brand, is a perfect illustration of the house's determination and talent for 'surprising without shocking'. Karl Lagerfeld, internationally renowned couturier, creates a new collection of luxurious fashion every season, never standing still and always reconciling Chanel style with cutting-edge creativity. Dominique Moncourtois and Heidi Morawetz, makeup and colour magicians, combine futuristic technology with house icons to create the glowing makeup of tomorrow. Fine Jewelry, always one of Chanel's greatest lines, produces top-of-the-range creations including Éléments Célestes, an avant-garde collection of exquisitely sumptuous jewels, faithful to the founder's love of diamonds. Coco Chanel was a woman of contrasts: discretion and extravagance, hyperbole and simplicity; she wanted 'to be part of the future' by devotedly – even ferociously – protecting everything she loved. Jacques Polge, perfumer, is a purveyor of mystery in the form of N° 5, one of Chanel's most legendary creations. He perpetuates the magic of the house fragrances and creates new perfumes that spread the myth, the miracle, the magic and the spirit of luxury to the four corners of the earth. This is Planet Chanel.

Danièle Bott

The spirit of Coco Chanel still reigns at the Place Vendôme (shown top). Very sure of her likes and dislikes, she was the arbiter of elegance throughout the 20th century. Portrait of Mademoiselle (above) by Boris Lipnitzki, July 1936.

'Luck is a way of being.
Luck is not a little person.
Luck is my soul.'

Gabrielle Chanel

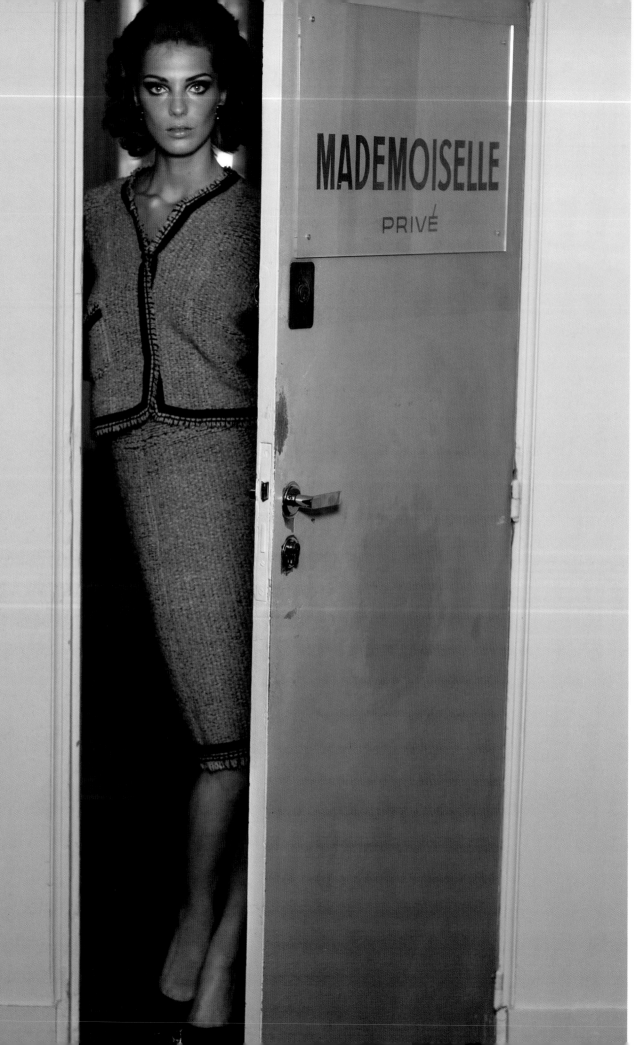

THE SUIT

'The art of couture is knowing how to enhance.'

The Chanel suit is ageless. A uniform of style, it is absolutely unique, resolutely modern, easy to wear and easy to personalize and recycle. The suit is associated with the woman who created *and* wore it for the first time in 1913, turning it into what she herself called the 'fashion statement of the century'. After almost ninety years of existence, the Chanel suit continues to be a timeless standard, eternally young. It is a phenomenon unaffected by the passing of time. Its story is the tale of a woman, a house, a style, a look which – updated, reinvented and subverted by Karl Lagerfeld, who has been with the house since 1983 – is now marching triumphant into the third millennium.

Few creations have had a greater influence on fashion than the Chanel suit. A classic symbol of French elegance, the suit is constructed according to a precise code: strict lines, a fitted cut articulated at exactly the right places to allow ease of movement; braid trimming on the jacket; sleeves fitted precisely at shoulder level; real pockets; an enduring range of colours – beige, navy blue, black, as well as pink, cherry red or pale green; a consistent choice of fabrics – jersey and tweeds or daring combinations, 'fabrics so dazzling as to strike the heartiest Highlander blind'.[1] The jackets and skirts are always cut from the same piece of fabric to avoid colour variations. The skirts are mounted on grosgrain at hip level, not on a waist-level belt, which would have resulted in unnecessary thickness. Braids and trimmings underline the contours of the jacket, redefine it, edge the pockets and cuffs, always with impeccable style. For Coco Chanel, luxury lay in invisible perfection.

The concept of a coordinated suit is believed to have been initially inspired by the first tailor-made suits for women created by English designer John Redfern in the late 19th century. From the very start, young Gabrielle Chanel imagined the suit in jersey, a fabric that society women of that period considered cheap and demeaning. Flexible, simple, comfortable, the suit was an expression, even a shout of defiance! As soon as she entered the world of fashion, Coco Chanel established herself as an ecumenical revolutionary, strongly opposed to the frou-frou of the *belle époque*, which was never her style.

Previous pages
A style statement, the incomparable look of a tweed suit with fringed trimmings. A 1960 Autumn–Winter design, styled and photographed by Karl Lagerfeld at the Creation Studio entrance (original door) for *Vogue* France, June–July 2004.

Opposite
A final fitting of Mademoiselle's emblematic suit for Ingrid Bergman, her costume for her role in *Tea and Sympathy* by Françoise Sagan, performed in Paris in December 1956. Photo from *Elle*, no. 17, December 1956.

By the time she arrived in Paris in 1907, before she was known as 'Mademoiselle', she was already noted for her schoolgirl ensembles: black smock, white lavallière with a velvet bow and 'orphan' shoes. 'I have very firm distastes',[2] she was soon to declare, borrowing a famous phrase from Jules Renard. She hated aigrettes, flounces, trains, lace, pastel chiffons and silks, all the ultra-feminine fineries that fashionable women were so fond of. 'I gave women's bodies their freedom back; their bodies sweated under all the showcase clothes, under their corsets, their underwear, their padding.'[3]

She wore clothes that she created herself, or rather clothes that she borrowed from men's tailoring or work clothes: jersey sailor tops for ease of movement, sports suits because she liked sport herself and didn't want to be hampered in her movements. Pleased with the results, she embraced the style with the determination of a pioneer. Just as sure of her likes as she was of her dislikes, she wanted to be 'part of the future'. Being the first to wear her own creations, she only wore and designed clothes she liked.

Gabrielle Chanel was inspired by the men in her life, but also by the places she liked to frequent, such as beaches, sporting venues and racetracks. Having moved in with horse breeder Étienne Balsan, the *irrégulière* as she was then known became a highly accomplished rider, and sported jodhpurs and a riding jacket. In a manner of speaking, the world of horse riding spurred her

visionary style, propelling her into the kingdom of fashion. Soon afterwards, in 1908, Balsan's apartment at 160 boulevard Malesherbes in Paris became her first millinery workshop. This is where she discovered her true self, where she soon felt she belonged. She was fascinated by Paris and high-society life.

Now it was her turn to seduce Paris. Before long, actresses and society ladies were at her feet. She visited only the most select places such as Maxim's and Lapérouse, where her portrait still attests to her frequent visits to

Previous pages
Chanel label on a suit
from the 1950s.

Opposite above
Fashion show in the
Couture 'Grand Salon',
rue Cambon. Photo by
Willy Rizzo for *Paris-Match*,
11 August 1956.

Right
A forerunner of the timeless
look: one of the first suits in
brown rayon with a fine
white check. The collar,
cuffs and lapels in white
piqué match the buttoned
top. 1935 Spring–Summer
creation. Photo Horst P.
Horst, for *Vogue* France.

Opposite
Suit in black ciré satin, finished with a large bow; blouse and jacket lining in white ciré satin; hat in black ciré satin. Photo published in *L'Officiel*, 1933.

Right
The total Chanel look: Vanessa Paradis wears a suit created in 1960, a perfect illustration of an enduring style. Photo by Karl Lagerfeld for the cover of *Marie-Claire*, October 2004, anniversary edition: 1954–2004.

Opposite

Signature details: woven
tweed with overstitched
trimmings outlining the
jacket, cuffs and pockets,
and gilt buttons. 2005
Spring–Summer Haute
Couture suit.

the private salons. She lived exclusively in fashionable districts: the 8th, the 17th and eventually the 1st arrondissement, home to her beloved Place Vendôme, where she loved to stroll.

'It was artists who taught me to be rigorous.'

Shortly after, 'Coco' Chanel as she was now known fell in love with Arthur Boy Capel, an extremely rich English businessman, the epitome of British elegance. As she often borrowed his suits, Boy, who admired her spirit, her vitality, her androgynous look and her very slim silhouette, suggested that she pay a visit to his tailor to 'make what she always wears elegant'.[4] With great daring – or was it simply perspicacity? – she agreed. Men's suits draped her with an elegance that was immediately recognized. With an adventurous spirit, she continued to explore the realm of men's clothes. First she liberated

jersey from its original function – underwear – then went on to adopt ties, sweaters, boaters, pea jackets, pyjamas and trousers. She simply felt comfortable in them. 'Rue Cambon grew from there,'[5] she later said.

Coco Chanel left the capital only to go to holiday resorts, where she adored the reinvigorating sea air and, above all, the dazzling sunshine. In Deauville in 1913, she opened up her first boutique specializing in holiday fashion and honed her philosophy: suitable clothes for every occasion, place and circumstance.

Jacques Prévert once said, 'A tomboy is a successful girl'. Coco Chanel embraced the idea long before these words were spoken: she wore wide-legged beach trousers, polo shirts or striped sailor tops, hid her already short hair under a turban, and introduced Deauville's aristocratic clientele to such items as bathing costumes, sportswear and long sweaters. In Biarritz, one of the last remaining luxury resorts in 1915, Chanel opened her first real couture house, where women flocked to buy her discreet, nouveau-chic garments that were suited to the times. Sensing that the war-stricken world was undergoing a major upheaval, Coco insisted on the need for new, truly functional clothes for women, clothes enabling them to move, work, walk and live as if in a second skin.

As early as 1917, the couturière was designing remarkably fluid garments, pairing long jackets with calf-length skirts, which provided – a novelty at that time – complete

freedom of movement. 'I was working for a changing society. Until then, fashion catered to useless ladies of leisure whose chambermaids had to help them put on their clothes. I now had a clientele of active women. Active women need to feel comfortable in their dresses, they need to be able to pull up their sleeves.'[6] She refused to make pockets so small you couldn't fit your hands in, did away with useless buttons, ensured skirts did not hinder walking and later shortened them. Designed to fit every occasion and function, her clothes were devoid of extravagant fineries. Indeed, Coco rejected showiness, and could still be heard criticizing it in 1959, in an interview with Pierre Dumayet for the famous French television show *Cinq Colonnes à la Une*.

Her first suits were worn with plain white blouses. The jackets had lapels or shawl collars, closed edge to edge and were fitted with pockets as big as those on a man's suit, while full or pleated skirts ensured comfort and ease. Made of fine-knit fabric, tweed, silk or velvet, the suit's radical simplicity immediately outclassed anything evoking *faux chic*. Chanel first came across tweed as far back as 1924, when her lover, the Duke of Westminster, took her to London. She chose this fabric primarily for its suppleness, for the way it 'subjugates light to shape'[7] but also for its woven palette of restrained colours that perfectly matched the skies and landscapes of England.

Was it at this time that she produced the first true Chanel suit? It's possible, for she was

already displaying a rare talent: the ability to take everything that she loved and match it to contemporary taste, making it unique, even desirable. Her way of wearing a garment, of dressing it up by adding accessories such as pearls, chains or flowers became a template for actresses and the fashionable elite who tried to copy her. One thing is sure: Coco Chanel was the first stylist.

She adored tweed, which satisfied all her requirements and became her favoured

Above
As beautiful inside as out: an entirely overstitched jacket lining, with gold chain sewn into the hem, to allow the fabric to hang perfectly.

Opposite
Time stands still for this perfectly modern suit in cotton granite with navy blue trimmings.
Photo Georges Saad, *L'Art et la Mode*, 1965.

Signature buttons: Coco Chanel was fond of gilt buttons embossed with a lion's head (her star sign was Leo), chains, stars, the sun, the double C or pearls. Following her lead, Karl Lagerfeld continues this tradition by decorating buttons with clover leaves, ears of wheat, bottles of Chanel N° 5 or even Mademoiselle's own profile.

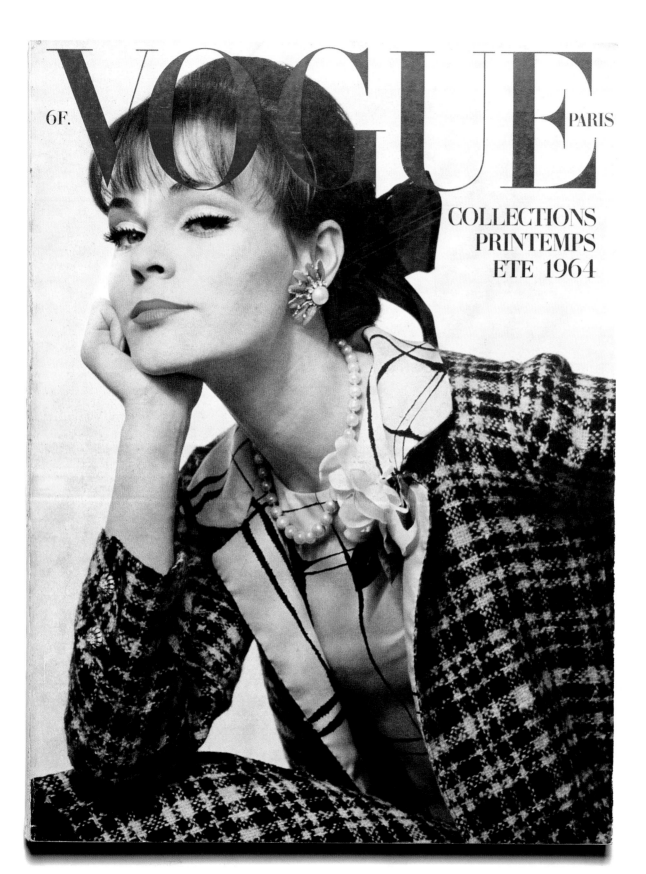

Left
White and navy blue
checked tweed. The blouse
matches the jacket lining.
Velvet hair bow and white
camellia. *Vogue* France
cover, March 1964.
Photo Helmut Newton.

Opposite
Suit in white knit with
braided wool brandenburgs
and trimmings in navy blue,
and matching boater.
Photo William Klein,
on the banks of the Seine.
Vogue France, 1960.

fabric. As usual, she had a very personal way of using it. 'I had the tweeds brought in from Scotland. Homespuns soon dethroned crêpe and chiffon. I got them to wash the wool less to keep it soft. In France, we wash too much. I asked the wholesalers for natural colours.'[8]

It is fascinating to discover that Coco Chanel never made any sketches. An artist to her very fingertips, she used scissors, pins and a live model to create her clothes, see them progress, feel them come to life, as if modelling clay. Unlike designers who design for ideal, goddess-like women, she created each garment for herself. A perfectionist, she constantly revised her designs, modified them, tweaked them, remodelled them, her sharp eyes detecting the slightest defect. She knew every point of articulation, every muscle of the body, and focused on the back, which she believed to be *the* strategic point in women's wear. Cardigans made of fine-knit jersey mixed with silk and edged with contrasting braid trimmings, knit or tweed suits over belted tunics, jacquard jackets with wrap skirts, blazers topped with a cloche hat: Coco Chanel, already an architect of style, created the look of the day.

When she made her comeback onto the fashion scene in 1954, she presented a new generation of suits, which soon emerged as the standard of elegance. Guided by her sound instinct and personal vision of the body, she relied on simplicity. The time was right; the new jeans and sweater trend was all the rage in the streets.

In keeping with her taste for ease and comfort, Mademoiselle 'sculpted' her clothes

'Nothing is more beautiful than freedom of the body.'

on the models themselves. Her 'absolute eye'[9] as Jean Cocteau called it, sought perfection in the construction of her suits, harmony in their proportions, balance in the way they hugged the lines of the body. She strove to create a garment that would fit like a second skin. She could spend hours trying to fit a sleeve, to the point of obsession. She would put it in place, take it off again, sometimes tear it off, fiddle with it, put it back. The sleeves were always made to measure to ensure a perfect fit for they were the key to elegance. Fixed high on the shoulder, at the outer tip of the collarbone, they seem narrow, even tight-fitting, but a piece of material under the armpit allows the sleeves to follow the movement of the arms, never to constrain them. Coco Chanel believed that sleeves were the quintessential expression of the art of couture. She was convinced that nothing was more important

Opposite
Mademoiselle's team of house models in Moscow, for the second Chanel show in Russia. Photo Trepetov, September 1967.

Opposite
This suit in navy blue jersey
embodies Coco Chanel's
beloved androgynous look.
1954 Spring–Summer
collection. Photo
Henry Clarke.

Above
Long redingote suit with
horseshoe neckline over
a two-tone dress in
black and white. 2003
Spring–Summer Haute
Couture collection.
Photo Karl Lagerfeld.

than ease and comfort, than respecting the
body's natural shapes. This can only be
achieved through patient work done by
hand, the use of refined fabrics, attention
to detail and accessories, and the kind of
masterful craftsmanship that only haute
couture can provide.

The suit's incomparable and sophisticated
elegance is just as visible on the inside as on
the outside. On and in a Chanel jacket, the
open, flattened, sometimes trimmed seams

are fixed into place by overcasting or
topstitching. The hems are made by
discreetly folding in the edge of the fabric
using the same overcast stitch. Sometimes,
the fabric's selvage – fixed to remain flat –
edges the bottom of the skirt and does away
with the need for a hem. Every detail is there
for a reason, every detail is important. For
instance, the gold chain along the hem of
the lining guarantees verticality and perfect
hang. It is also a true trademark of Chanel,
the only couture house to 'weight' its jackets
in this way. The blouses often match the
jacket lining to create an effect of top-to-toe
harmony. Just like the 2-55 quilted bag
created in February 1955, overstitching has
become a fashion trademark; it was initially
applied to the very first suits to make sure
the jersey jackets kept their shape without
affecting their lightness, comfort and
flexibility. In fact, quilting is a technique that
Coco Chanel borrowed from the jackets
worn by stable boys at the racetracks. The
trick is to join the suit lining and fabric by
stitching them together vertically to prevent
the jacket from losing its shape. The
buttonholes are never fake and the silk
linings always bear the house logo, which
Karl Lagerfeld reintroduced as soon as he
arrived at rue Cambon. The buttons are
designed to resemble jewelry. For each
collection, the designs change: the double C,
a four-leaf clover, a star, small chains, the
sun, ears of wheat – they all recall
Mademoiselle's favourite symbols. The head
of the lion, for example, represents her star
sign, Leo. Karl Lagerfeld carries on adorning
the buttons with his usual playfulness,

Opposite
The Chanel look embodied by Coco's favourite model, Marie-Hélène Arnaud. Chiné tweed suit in beige and brown. Long-sleeved shantung blouse with removable cuffs. Mademoiselle loved this outfit and wore it herself. Photo Sante Forlano, *Vogue* France 1958.

Right
Chanel ambassadress Anna Mouglalis in a cardigan-style jacket in checked tweed, teamed with a pair of simple jeans. With a double strand of pearls and black velvet bow, this is the look adopted by the new generation of 'Chanel girls'. Cover of *Elle*, 25 November 2002. Photo Karl Lagerfeld.

Left
Absolute elegance: a
suit in navy blue braided
wool enlivened by cravat
and cuffs in white silk.
Notable details include
patch pockets and
narrow shoulders.
Photo Helmut Newton,
Elle, September 1968.

Opposite
Anthracite jersey knit,
Mademoiselle's favourite
fabric, for this strict and
simple suit. Photo Sabine
Weiss for *Vogue* France,
November 1956.

embracing all the house symbols: small mirrors, camellias, bags, shoes, bottles of N° 5, mostly hand-crafted by the Desrues ateliers. Branding, wit, charm and fun are a constant on these novel buttons, which have become a house trademark. All these trade secrets, symbols and iconic details constitute a body of knowledge that grows ever richer.

'I always finish my collections at the last minute. The day before the show, I am capable of changing everything if a detail bothers me, or if I have the impression that

'*I wanted to make women conform to nature.*'

everything is already out of date!', Coco Chanel confided to Pierre Dumayet in February 1959. And yet, nothing looks more like a Chanel suit than a Chanel suit. For Coco Chanel, who was to be hailed as one of France's greatest couturiers of the century, fashion changed but style remained. When Mademoiselle made her comeback to rue Cambon in 1954, she took the incredible risk of taking up her creations where she had left off just before 1939 when, tired and alone, she had exiled herself to Switzerland. Passionate and unyielding, she once more

gave out her orders, and reinvented a vision that was still her own. She designed for active women who are always on the move, even when they seem static. Comfort, wrongly considered to be the opposite of elegance, remained the key to the look epitomized by the Chanel style. She created the total Chanel look without a notion that the phrase would later be used in a critical sense. A tweed suit with a below-the-knee skirt, a quilted bag, gold chain belts, boater, two-tone slingbacks, pale stockings and ever-present camellia, Coco's philosophy became a fashion statement.

Mademoiselle's obstinate refusal to be ostentatious, her sense of moderation and her penchant for classicism naturally inspired her to create easy-to-wear clothes. Just as naturally, she chose her models for their innate elegance, women who, like her, had no wish to feel dressed up. She recruited her models – including Marie-Hélène Arnaud, Odile de Crouy and Gisèle Franchomme – from among her friends, connections and the high-society women who abhorred eccentricity and the pointless and uncomfortable dictates of fashion.

Before long, all the stars were sporting Chanel, so much so that the tweed jacket became synonymous with a certain era of cinema. Romy Schneider wore a matching

Opposite
Incomparable Chanel model Suzy Parker.
Photo Horst P. Horst, 1964.

Irina, on the beige suede couch in Mademoiselle's home at rue Cambon, wearing a suit composed of a navy blue and white checked tweed jacket and dress. *Marie-Claire* Latin America, October 2004. Photo Oleg Covian.

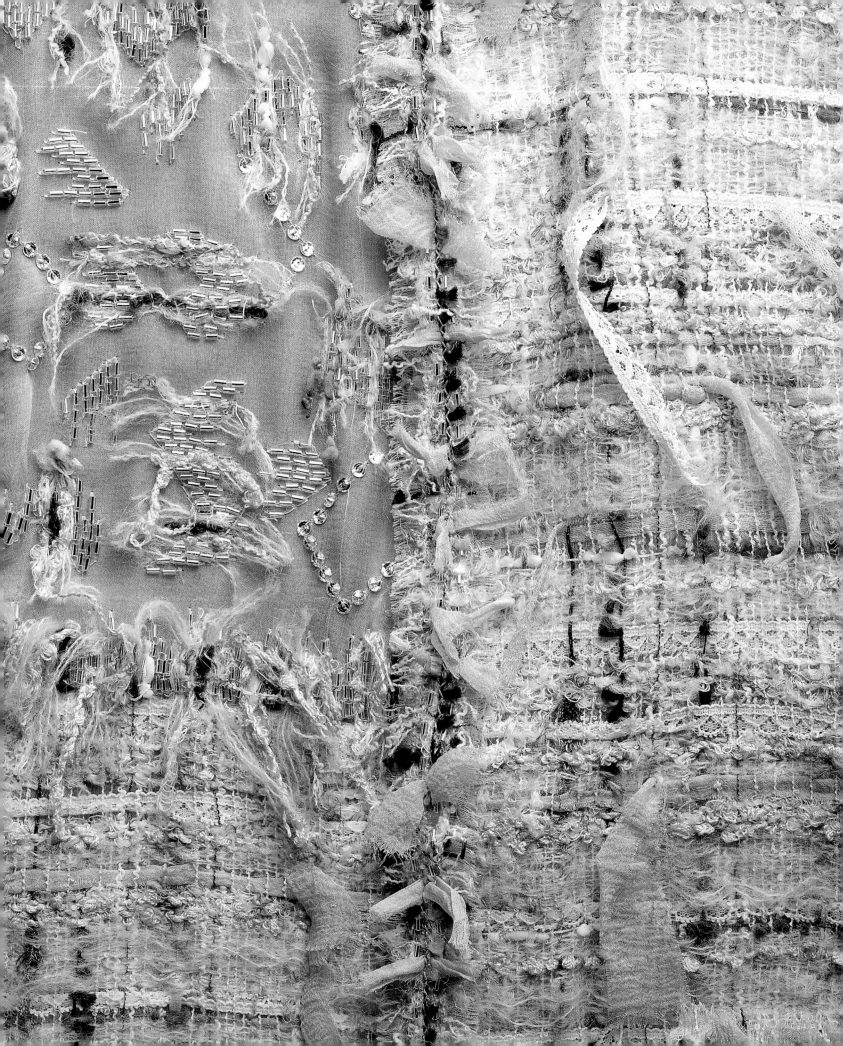

Opposite
Contemporary variations on
tweed: woven, frayed and
encrusted with beads.

Right
A cascade of necklaces,
a boater poised on an
impossible hairstyle, and
cherry red buttons for this
pastel speckled tweed suit
with 'disintegrating' hemline
on tulle. A Karl Lagerfeld
creation for 2003
Spring–Summer Chanel
Haute Couture. Photo
Karl Lagerfeld.

suit and fur hat in Visconti's segment of *Boccaccio '70*, Jeanne Moreau donned a checked tweed suit and a plain black one bearing the signature camellia in Roger Vadim's *Les Liaisons Dangereuses*. Marlene Dietrich wore an ultra-sophisticated striped organza suit. All the beautiful Frenchwomen of the day, including Anouk Aimée, Françoise Arnoul and Micheline Presle, flocked to Chanel to discover those 'friendly' suits that fitted like a second skin. Jackie Kennedy made the suit internationally – and tragically – famous, while the French First Lady, Claude Pompidou, wore it like a uniform, as did several other female politicians. The Chanel suit was so obviously the perfect choice, suitable for all occasions, that it risked being labelled 'bourgeois' for the first time in its history.

When Coco Chanel passed away, it was thought that the mythical Chanel style might die out. But in 1983, designer Karl Lagerfeld was appointed Artistic Director of the celebrated fashion house and breathed new life into the brand by conveying his passion for contemporary luxury. Hailed emperor of fashion, this erudite, post-modern dandy, creator of illusions of beauty, driven by insatiable curiosity and creativity, declares that he merely obeys his instinct, the spirit of the period and his perpetual desire for change. Possibly perceiving in Coco Chanel

some of the character traits of his own mother who 'could not bear the slightest error of taste',[10] Karl Lagerfeld presents ten Chanel collections every season. Given his experience in the field of fashion together with his knowledge of couture techniques and highly sophisticated craftsmanship, he has a background few designers can equal. Despite his claims that 'the past is but an illusion',[11] and that only his new creations count, he nonetheless continues to draw on and transfigure the classic suit. From Vanessa Paradis to Anna Mouglalis, to Kate Moss or

'Every decision is a refusal.'

Spinoza, quoted by Karl Lagerfeld

Uma Thurman, today's 'Chanel Girls' embrace the Chanel suit with ritualistic reverence, succumbing to its charms, and revelling in it without restraint. The fringed tweed jacket worn over a pair of jeans is the latest version of an enduring style, proof that the signature suit has survived all the upheavals of the past fifty years without losing its identity.

But the greatest paradox of all – or is it a sign of loyalty? – is that Karl Lagerfeld never stops quoting these distinctive

Opposite
Inès de La Fressange in a quilted suit, embroidered with self-coloured sequins and trimmed with a chain motif that recalls the iconic 2-55 bag. 1986 Autumn–Winter Haute Couture. Photo Gilles Bensimon.

symbols, giving them an ironic twist. Every one of his collections highlights the house icons in his own personal way. 'Absolute respect would have been fatal to creativity', he has often said. 'I took the Chanel codes, or language, and I mixed them up. Mademoiselle's basic idea was timeless modernity. But my job was primarily to reinvent Chanel. So I played with the codes, manipulated them, sometimes even eliminated them before bringing them back. Fashion is not respect; it is first and foremost fashion. I don't like nostalgia. At times, my "reinventions" shocked the purists who thought I was destroying Mademoiselle's elegant simplicity. But I was not afraid.' Through this daring, this irreverence and this taste for self-mockery and fantasy, these countless variations result in dazzling creativity, pure and simple. Every one of Lagerfeld's collections – a combination of surprise, sumptuous luxury and witty nods to modern times – is a much-awaited event.

If we go back in time, a revised and remodelled version of the suit is always the catwalk star of the year. In 1986 it was in a demure, quilted version with ribbon-chain trimming worn by Inès de la Fressange, the house ambassadress of the day. A few years later, it reappeared but was completely different once again. The perfectly proportioned jacket may be shown with a long or short skirt, slacks, capri pants, city shorts or leggings. It appears in a wide range of tweeds: dark or pastel colours, chiné, checked, mixed, fringed or lamé. The suit has become a garment where everything is possible, reinterpreted by the visionary skills of a magician; an expression of passion from a couturier who loves luxury, improvisation and freedom.

Flounces, lace, guipure, prints, tulle, knit or transparent fabrics become his 'signature card' of the season. Everyone is inspired by his designs, and the Chanel suit *à la* Karl Lagerfeld is probably one of the most copied

Opposite
Austere suit in wool crêpe, with a flared skirt over 'mushroom' petticoats in pleated and embroidered tulle. 2002 Haute Couture collection. Photo Karl Lagerfeld.

Right
In fringed tweed and a loosely tied cravat, top model Daria was the key figure in the 2005 Spring–Summer Boutique catalogue. Photo Karl Lagerfeld.

Opposite

The return of sophistication with this sequinned tweed suit, 2005 Spring–Summer Haute Couture. Photo Karl Lagerfeld.

Right

White cotton sleeveless dress, knitted in the style of a traditional bedcover. Soft tweed cardigan embellished with white crochet trimmings. 2004 Spring–Summer Prêt-à-Porter. Photo Karl Lagerfeld.

A vision of style: Daria in pastel tweed at the entrance of the Chanel boutique. 2005 Spring–Summer catalogue. Photo Karl Lagerfeld.

in the world. When the variations begin to stray too far from the original model, the designer simply reverts to the sobriety of the original, to the acclaim and appreciation of all. We see the return of black and white, simple checked tweed, the neo-tuxedo jacket. But what is bred in the bone comes out in the flesh, and his imagination will soon take flight once again, with that dizzying sensation of freedom so characteristic of this master of design. The 2004 Spring–Summer collection featured a soft tweed cardigan jacket with white crochet trimmings over a cotton dress, knitted in the style of a traditional bedcover, and a gypsy skirt paired with a knit jacket. Buttons and other details are constantly revamped and turned into objects of desire in themselves, giving the silhouette that iconic touch.

For Chanel, couture is the house's principal vocation. For Karl Lagerfeld, it means the privilege of not having to think about price. Dedicated to perfection and concerned about the future and the legacy of haute couture, Chanel has recently bought six ateliers that have long worked with the rue Cambon house: Massaro for shoes, Lemarié for feathers and camellias, Michel for hats, Desrues for haberdashery (chains, buttons) and Lesage for embroidery. It was in the Lesage workshop that the first samples of

'reworked' tweed were tested seven years ago. 'In the early days,' explains Mr François Lesage, 'the threads were twisted together, recalling a luxurious mop. Today the work done on tweeds in the couture embroidery workshops is amazing: sequins, feathers, braids and trimmings and even crystal splinters provide an endless array of garnishes. The result is a stunning fabric that Karl Lagerfeld uses for both his Prêt-à-Porter and Haute Couture collections.' Only a

'A fashion that does not make one look up-to-date is not a fashion.'

leading house like Chanel could inspire – and fund – such a level of creative productivity. Even more recently, the ranks were swelled by the addition of Goossens, whose baroque jewels once mesmerized Mademoiselle. Even back in 1958, she already sensed that these workshops and their '*petites mains*' might disappear and feared for their future. By safeguarding these crafts, so crucial to the success of the sumptuous collections, Chanel Haute Couture remains ahead of the times.

THE CAMELLIA

'There are a hundred ways to wear a flower.'

Twenty-five voluptuous petals wound in a spiral, a sensuous centre, a line inscribed within a circle, sensual sophistication, romance tinged with the eroticism that once enchanted the 'sublime masochist' and literary heroine Marguerite Gautier: the camellia was the favourite flower of Coco Chanel – one of the most demanding women of her century – to the extent of becoming a fetish, the perfect symbol of subtle androgynous femininity, the very image of Coco's creations.

Pinned nonchalantly but strikingly to the buttoned belt of a jersey suit composed of a sailor top with large pockets and a long skirt, the virginal flower made its first discreet appearance back in 1913. Was this the first Chanel camellia or just a simple flower? Gabrielle Chanel, wearing a lavallière, her hair parted down the middle and tied up in a bun, strolled along Etretat beach in Normandy and smiled, as if amused by this discreet allusion to seduction, spiced with ambiguity.

The camellia, an exotic, forbidden flower, comes from a family of native Asian shrubs with shiny evergreen oval-shaped leaves and luxuriantly blooming flowers. There are thought to be about 120 different varieties of camellia, known in Asia as the 'Japanese rose'. It is mainly cultivated as an ornamental plant.

A symbol of carnal desire, camellias arrived in Europe in the mid-19th century. In France under Louis-Philippe and in Tsarist Russia, the immaculate white flower, so voluptuous yet radiant with purity, accentuated the beauty of women, flattered their décolletés and adorned their hair. Both aristocratic and society women adored them. They donned the flower as a sign of seduction and flirtatiousness, an erotic signal much like the black velvet beauty patches or *mouches* that 18th-century *belles dames* wore next to their lips or high on their cheekbones. Camellias were part of the socialite scene – at the theatre, at the opera, on carriage rides in the Bois de Boulogne, they became the emblem of women seeking to seduce, often frivolous, artificial, even shocking.

The scandal-scented camellia was immortalized by Alexandre Dumas fils, who wrote *La Dame aux Camélias* (*The Lady of the Camellias*), inspired by the life of the courtesan Marie Duplessis. Dumas's heroine,

Previous pages and opposite, background
Positive/negative camellia motif on a fabric created for Chanel in 1934.

Opposite, inset
The timeless style of Coco Chanel, captured in a portrait by Man Ray, 1935.

Marguerite Gautier, sacrifices her love and dies of consumption, becoming the epitome of passionate romance. Soon after, Dumas adapted his novel into a highly successful and popular play which has been performed and reinterpreted by the greatest actresses, from Sarah Bernhardt to Isabelle Adjani. In his opera *La Traviata*, inspired by the play, Verdi transformed the heroine he renamed Violetta Valéry into an icon of love and passion.

Of course, Coco Chanel had nothing in common with these romantic heroines doomed to be martyrs to love, and even less with professional courtesans! Barely two years after founding her couture house, she refused to let her friend and protector, Boy Capel, continue helping her. She was much more drawn to work than to money and soon proved to be a shrewd businesswoman. There was no question of depending on a man for financial support. More than anything, she valued her hard-won freedom, a freedom she was to defend at every turn.

In the twenties, Proust, a Dumas enthusiast and ardent admirer of *La Traviata*, flaunted a camellia at the Salon de Guermantes, at a time when elegant young men sported carnations or gardenias on their lapels. Before long, it became the emblem of a new generation of dandies who casually pinned a camellia on their jackets. Coco Chanel, very much inspired by masculine clothes, borrowed the flower from these men. She was enchanted by its perfect, almost geometric roundness. What was it that gave her the idea of pinning a single white camellia on her

'What do you eat for breakfast?'

'Madame, I eat a camellia, and in the evening I eat an orchid.'

black dress for the first time? Was it perhaps a bouquet of camellias she received from the Duke of Westminster or another of her admirers? We will never know.

The camellia possessed the added advantage of not competing with her favourite perfume – camellias are scentless. This is why it was replaced by the very fragrant gardenia in her perfume creations. But one thing is certain: she was instantly captivated by the contrast of white on black, the effects of light and shade she favoured throughout her career.

Previous pages
The versatile camellia in all its splendour… and in all materials: silk, organza, rhodoid, raffia, sequins, leather, chiffon and feathers. The Lemarié ateliers make 20,000 flowers a year.

Opposite
Camellia branches decorate a Coromandel screen in the hall of Mademoiselle's rue Cambon apartment.

Opposite
The immaculate glow of a camellia against dark hair. A 1961 creation. Photo Willy Rizzo.

Right
A bewitching web of camellias, from the 2000 Haute Couture Spring–Summer fashion show. Photo Frédérique Dumoulin.

Previous page, left
Detail of golden camellias
embroidered on a dress.
2005 Spring–Summer Haute
Couture collection.

Previous page, right
Model with a camellia, seen
on the famous mirror-lined
stairway at rue Cambon.
Photo François Kollar 1937
for *Harper's Bazaar.*

Opposite
Massaro sandals and shoes
with camellias embroidered
by Lesage for Chanel.

Coco Chanel believed that beauty is nearly always born from radical simplicity. The camellia, with its minimalist lines, well-defined voluptuous curves and almost Art Nouveau design was destined to appeal to her as an aesthete and as an avant-garde designer. She loved white and made it one of her signature colours because it evoked harmony, pure light, perfect and sensual beauty, restrained emotions, asceticism but also sumptuous simplicity.

The camellia became Coco's symbol, her icon, one of the recurring elements of her style. However, Mademoiselle did not merely use it as an accessory in its natural form. As always when drawn to a particular shape, colour or garment, she truly made it her own, and interpreted it in unexpected ways in her designs. We find a stylized camellia embroidered on a blouse as far back as 1922. Later, the motif is delicately poised on the strap of a black chiffon dress with a long scarf, 'suitable for both travel and town wear', created in 1924. Then in 1927, a camellia in white piqué adds a lovely decorative touch to a simple grey coat with a dropped-waist belt. That same year, a camellia braid highlights the back décolleté of a simple black dress, adorned with a hint of guipure lace, the ultimate in refinement. By the thirties, the timeless camellia was appearing in restrained black and white prints.

A motif, an ornament, an accessory and above all, a style trademark, the camellia enlivens a belt or decorates a collar. Coco Chanel also continued to pin the pure white flower onto her sophisticated black dresses or sweaters. Already resembling the one we recognize today, the camellia made its first official appearance on a black suit with white trim in 1933.

Mademoiselle liked to be surrounded by lucky charms and symbols, and also featured her favourite flower in her own home. In the

'A lot of serious work goes into successful frivolity.'

hall of her apartment at 31 rue Cambon, there are inlaid camellia branches on her famous Coromandel lacquered screen dating back to the Kangxi period (1680 to 1720), the golden age for the Chinese folding screens that she adored. In her office, the elegant flower mingles with acanthus leaves to decorate a Venetian crystal chandelier. Elsewhere, highly stylized camellias festoon other chandeliers and mirrors, like a musical

motif, constantly repeated in a neverending stream of variations.

The year is 1936, and Coco Chanel poses for Sir Cecil Beaton's camera in a long embroidered lace dress and gold chain belt. A camellia adorns the veil on her head, adding a sophisticated touch to her pitch-black hair, styled with characteristic simplicity. As if in tribute to her beauty, two sculpted black servant boys wearing turbans, recalling the similar statues that stood in her hallway, each offer her a camellia. In another image, from 1937, with a cigarette between her lips, a black hair band, strings of pearls, sautoirs, cuff bracelets and a large white camellia pinned on the lapel of her checked tweed jacket, Mademoiselle symbolizes the Chanel look with supreme elegance.

It is in 1938 that the camellia blossoms into a piece of jewelry, in the delicate form of a necklace made from translucent glass, hand-crafted in the Gripoix ateliers. By 1954, the emblematic flower decorates the hairstyles created by Alexandre for the Chanel collections. Fashion at the time may have favoured long hair tied back with a bow, but top model Marie-Hélène Arnaud made a huge impact with an elegant, very contemporary short cut with just a touch of body, and she became the living incarnation of the Chanel look of that period. In fact, Chanel's star model was said to resemble Mademoiselle herself. The flower, precariously pinned on her dark hair with auburn tints, accents the base of her perfectly smooth fringe. Decorating a hair bow worn by Suzy Parker, the most renowned cover girl

of the period, or a headband, the camellia changed its role, coming to define a style. A boater, a suit with gilt buttons, one or more camellias, a gold chain belt, a quilted bag, pale stockings, two-tone pumps: all the iconic features of the timeless Chanel look were now firmly in place. The classic style is highlighted by sophisticated accessories or carefully chosen jewelry, acting as a counterpoint. According to Roland Barthes, 'a detached term (a pocket, a flower, a scarf, a piece of jewelry) holds the power of signification: a truth that is not only analytical but poetic.'[1]

An essential element in Mademoiselle's collections, the camellia is now reworked and reinterpreted by Karl Lagerfeld who includes it in his design vocabulary as a hallmark, an echo of the past revisited, a playful allusion to the house style. He constantly subverts its role, gives it a creative twist. The camellia stars in every catwalk show, always present, always surprising. Lagerfeld improvises like a musician, remodelling the camellia in every imaginable way, reinventing and redesigning it every season, recycling it in all sizes and all fabrics in every one of his annual collections. In couture, accessories and fine jewelry, in every material – satin, velvet, leather, rhodoid, canvas, tulle, chiffon and tweed – the camellia is the spirit of fashion; it works in every colour and grows more

Previous pages
The camellia, adapted to adorn a whole range of signature bags. The 2-55 bag has now celebrated over fifty years of success.

Opposite
White and black silk camellias: the very essence of style.

seductive with every adaptation. The camellia adorns everything, turns up everywhere: stitched on a boater, on the latest suit of the season, on the most sumptuous evening gown, in the hair of Vanessa Paradis and Nicole Kidman, on the fingers of Carole Bouquet… the camellia is everywhere. Interpreted as a simple, single flower, or more recently, as a many-fronded corsage in diaphanous chiffon, worked in sequins on a silk bag or a pair of evening shoes; in costume jewelry made of Bakelite, porcelain or gold, it lies at the heart of every accessory collection. The camellia is seduction itself, a fashion essential, a lucky charm among the other icons of Chanel.

In the 2004–2005 Autumn–Winter pre-collection, a rhinestone camellia adorns a satin sandal. In an accessory collection from the same season, a fluorescent version lights up a lightweight black nylon bag, while another glows on a black leather bag with red overstitching. It is subtly woven into the tweed fabric of another bag, where its delicate pastel colours seem to make it part of nature. Even when it is barely visible, it somehow remains fundamental.

In the fashion collections, a multitude of ethereal camellias in matching tones of red are embroidered onto a two-piece chiffon print evening gown with a train. The train itself is edged with a garden of camellias, fit for a beautiful princess. The same 2003 Spring–Summer collection features an evening dress in white chiffon speckled with coral, embellished with a flurry of camellia petals embroidered on a tulle base with a 'disintegrating' hem. Elsewhere, a train of flowers creates a romantic silhouette, while from a dark chignon streams a provocative cascade of dazzling blooms, fixed by a rhinestone camellia. A red camellia brooch features as a beauty accessory (just as Coco Chanel might have used it, for she knew how

'Black comprises everything. So does white. They possess absolute beauty. They are in perfect harmony.'

flattering red was to the face), shining as radiantly as a lipstick when pinned on a tomato-red cashmere cardigan with frayed, lettuce-green knit trimmings.

Woven into tweed, overstitched onto a top – a true work of art – composed only of tiny candy-coloured tulle camellias; on a skirt, a lace dress, or on a glamorous white and pink tulle sheath, this iconic flower lights up every

Opposite
A subtle, sinuous lace sheath entirely encrusted with camellias. Photo Karl Lagerfeld for 2002 Spring–Summer Chanel Haute Couture.

Opposite
Mademoiselle stands next
to a Venetian statue of a
Moor, like those in her
rue Cambon apartment.
Photograph by Cecil
Beaton, 1936.

Right
Fabric motif created for
Chanel in 1934.

Opposite
Eternal icons of Chanel, reinterpreted by Karl Lagerfeld. Sketch by Karl Lagerfeld, 2002.

Right
Camellia brooch in 18-carat white gold with 171 white diamonds, including a 2.5-carat diamond in the centre, and 992 black diamonds for a total weight of 55 carats. Chanel Fine Jewelry.

'We seem to forget that couture is a craft.'

runway show. A byword for luxury, the camellia has been featured more strongly than ever in the latest Haute Couture collections. The concept of the chain, another Chanel symbol, was paired with the ever-present camellia to create some absolutely stunning – and daringly experimental – embroidery on a series of ultra-feminine dresses. This was achieved by creating embroidered camellia motifs from delicate chains (skilfully oxidized to make them practically invisible) and then inlaying them into the garment fabric itself. This surprising technique is a perfect illustration of how the camellia can be treated with futuristic modernism. The 2005 Autumn–Winter collection offered another fabulous creation: a wedding dress strewn with almost four thousand camellias handcrafted by Lemarié and embroidered by Lesage, two of rue Cambon's satellite ateliers. This fairytale dress took seven hundred hours to create – enough to set the whole world dreaming.

Next stop, Place Vendôme, home to Chanel's Fine Jewelry. Here, the camellia is the source of inspiration for a line of enchanting pieces created with precious materials: rings featuring cacholong, onyx, aquamarine, peridot or black diamonds, or a 'secret' watch in white gold and diamonds mounted on a bracelet of cultured pearls. The camellia has blossomed into a timeless jewel.

To return to the original flower, what ateliers, what skilled artisans lie behind the countless camellias? The man responsible for these treasures, dubbed '*l'homme aux camélias*' by Karl Lagerfeld, is Monsieur Lemarié. He runs the Lemarié atelier, one of the last surviving flower and feather workshops – there were 277 such workshops in 1946. Backed by versatile, highly qualified craftsmen, the atelier is capable of fulfilling the designer's every whim. The longstanding savvy and craftsmanship of this unique workshop is essential in creating haute couture magic. The house of Chanel, seeking to preserve this threatened heritage, bought up the workshop founded more than a century ago by Palmyre Coyette, André Lemarié's grandmother, when feather hats were all the rage. The atelier's legacy encompasses a host of hidden treasures, tucked away in huge drawers full of secrets: feathers of now protected species including herons, birds of paradise and others which can no longer be used are now replaced by goose, swan, peacock and guinea-fowl feathers, all of which can be dyed, shaped and metamorphosed in a million ways.

Opposite
The camellia printed on
a knitted check fabric,
2005 Autumn–Winter
Prêt-à-Porter.

Right
'Camélia Secret' watch in
white gold and diamonds
on a black satin strap
bracelet set with diamonds.
Chanel Watches.

A camellia hair bun
created backstage by
Odile Gilbert for the
2000 Spring–Summer
Haute Couture collection.
Photo Capella.

Opposite
Artist Salvador Dali and
Coco Chanel: two friends
sharing a relaxed moment.

Right
A magnificent many-fronded
camellia in featherweight
chiffon. 2004 Spring–
Summer Haute Couture.

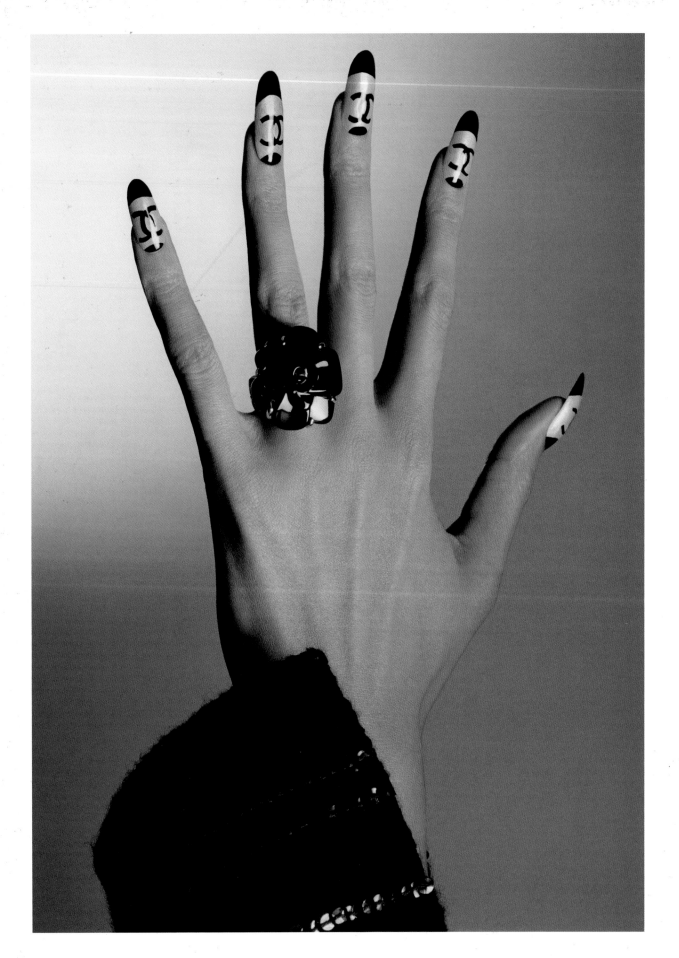

Left
Lacquered false nails
bearing the Chanel logo.
2001 Cruise Collection.
Camellia ring in yellow
18-carat gold and onyx.
Photo Isabelle Bonjean.
Chanel Fine Jewelry.

Opposite
Punctuating a perfect line:
the camellia highlights a
pale pink suit from 1963.
Photo David Bailey,
published in *Vogue*
France, September 1963.

Every year, more than twenty thousand camellias are handcrafted in Lemarié's flower and feather atelier, now a star in the Chanel galaxy. The confection of these versatile camellias requires deft skill and exacting precision. With mastery and expertise, the nimble-fingered workers make every single camellia entirely by hand, working at aged wood tables in keeping with a century-old ritual. Today's camellia often bears little resemblance to Mademoiselle's original flowers because of the diversity of the fabrics used by Karl Lagerfeld, but the basic design of this mythical blossom continues to echo with the Chanel spirit. Whether a classic version in pongé silk or glazed cotton, or a contemporary one in chiné or lamé tweeds, mohair, cashmere, denim, satin, velvet, tulle, chiffon or lace, or an offbeat version in leather, rhodoid, python, kangaroo, rabbit or even daring interpretations in cardboard or tin, the camellia seems to unleash boundless creativity every season. Everything is possible: all kinds of fabric combinations, all kinds of contrasts, all kinds of fantasies – fringed trims, sequins, embroideries… No two camellias are alike, not a single collection uses last season's creations. Sometimes, 15 centimetres of fabric measuring 90 to 130 centimetres in width is enough to make three or four camellias – what precision, what sophistication and elegance in the cutting, the mounting, the finishing!

No matter what material has been chosen, the four stages that go into crafting a signature flower are always the same. First, the fabric is dressed, the petals are then cut out after which they are individually shaped over a white-hot ball, using a technique developed in the late 19th century. Lastly, the flower is assembled by overlapping each petal, and fixed onto a tiny stem with a brass wire. It takes anywhere from twenty minutes to an hour and a half to complete a flower. Trickiest of all is the technique which consists of fraying or fringing a tweed camellia, especially when different tweeds are used and the fringed strips have to be stuck directly on the flower. In that case, the amount of time spent on each flower is impossible to calculate. But the ultimate in sophistication is the transparent fronded camellias created for the 2004 Spring–Summer Haute Couture collection, each of which took two hours to make! The result is an exquisite multitiered masterpiece in pastel chiffon, composed of more than fifteen layers, trailing its long, floating fronds – a work of chimerical beauty, recalling delicate clouds, those 'marvellous clouds' from the poetry of Baudelaire, a dream world of unabashed femininity.

Opposite
Wedding dress encrusted with 2,000 camellias. This masterpiece was the star of the 2005 Spring–Summer Haute Couture collection.

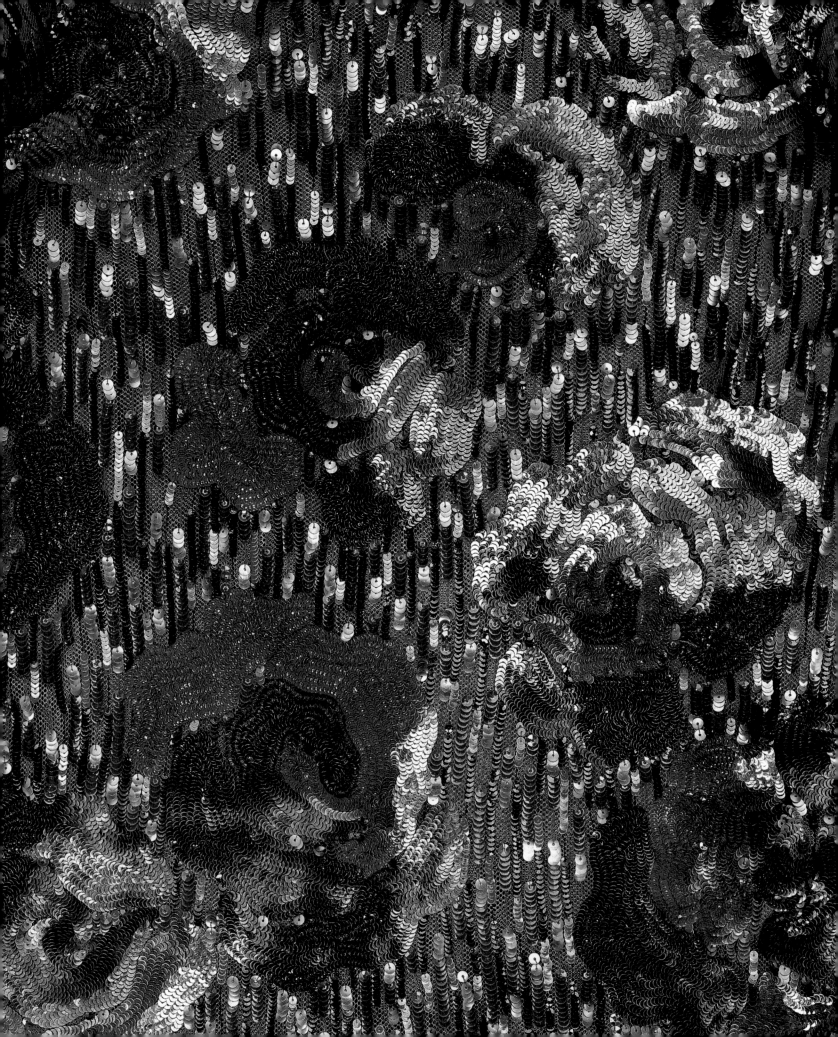

Opposite
Tweed sequinned and
embroidered by Lesage,
a Chanel 'satellite' atelier.

Right
A sumptuous 'bird of
paradise': Vanessa Paradis
models a pink marabout
cape created in 1926. In
her hair, a camellia brooch
in 18-carat white gold, with
a 2.51-carat diamond,
934 pink sapphires for a
total weight of 72 carats
and 194 white diamonds.
Photo Karl Lagerfeld.

JEWELRY

'My jewels represent an idea, first and foremost! I wanted to cover women with constellations.'

In the early 1930s, Coco Chanel, the queen of audacity, who until then had exalted the pure forms of classicism *à la française*, allowed herself a moment of contrition. A woman of contrasts who had previously designed only costume jewelry, 'because it was devoid of arrogance in an era of overly easy luxury'[1] and criticized in no uncertain terms the ostentatious glitter of real jewelry, Mademoiselle now exhibited the most sumptuous, exuberant and phantasmagorical collection of diamonds ever, for all of Paris to see. That day, 1 November 1932, marked a turning point. In the private rooms of her *hôtel particulier* at 29 rue du Faubourg-Saint-Honoré, with its 'high ceilings and golden wood panelling, evocative of a luxurious past',[2] Mademoiselle presented her first fine jewelry collection. Lacquered screens, antique furniture – Mademoiselle chose the intimacy of her own home to display these jewels on simple wax models with impeccably made-up stylized faces. Their painted-on smiles created a presence, a kind of authenticity, an impression of complicity with the public. Jewels sparkled in their dark hair, on their bare shoulders, around their throats; gems the likes of which had never been seen before, heavenly pieces entirely set with the most extraordinary and beautiful diamonds. So-called 'afternoon' jewelry was pinned on berets, fur hats and capes. The initial reaction of visitors was one of amazement followed by absolute fascination. Mesmerized, they could not take their eyes off the constellations, comets, cascades of stars, crescent moons! Never had a jewelry exhibition shown such sumptuous luxury, displayed such marvellous jewels, aroused so much curiosity: all through the month of November 1932, more than 30,000 visitors came to admire Mademoiselle's jewels, which were the talk of Paris society! At that time, their value was estimated at 93 million francs. What daring, what outrageous splendour! But Chanel, in *grande dame* style, donated all the money received in entrance fees to charity.

What had happened to convince Coco Chanel to exhibit these designs, which seemed to contradict everything that she had stated previously? What was her reasoning? What was its origin? Was it just a whim? A need to astonish, to show another facet of her talent? In fact, the explanation is quite simple. Mademoiselle never took any

Previous pages
'Franges' necklace, a reissue of an original 1932 design, worn here as a tiara. White gold set with 695 diamonds: diamond fringe composed of 627 diamonds mounted on a neck chain made of 68 diamonds.

Opposite
Coco Chanel on the balcony of her Ritz apartment in 1935. Chanel Fine Jewelry moved to the former Hôtel de Cressart at 18 place Vendôme on 18 November 1997. Photo Roger Schall.

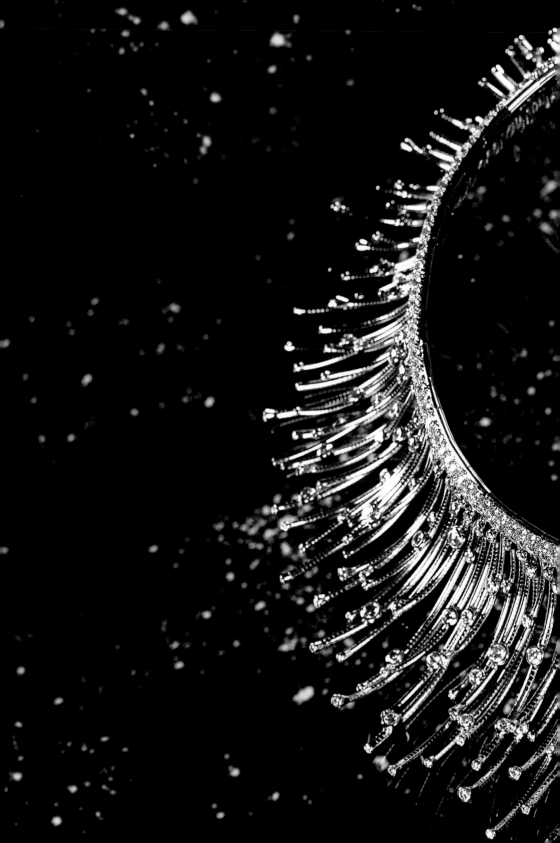

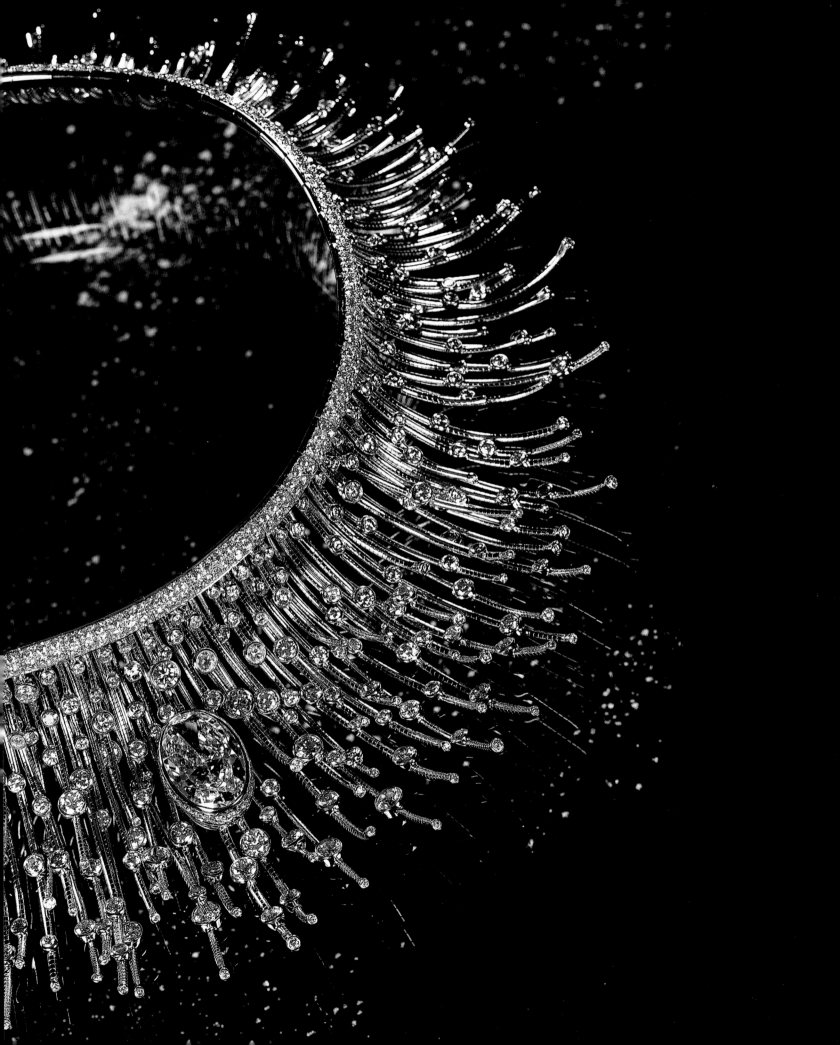

decisions lightly. Her work was one of her main reasons for living, and in that regard, she trusted no one but herself, only her own ideas, her instinct as a woman of fashion, of acumen, of business. She had accepted a request from the International Diamond Guild to work with this precious stone and help them boost their sales at a time of economic depression, and had made this choice because 'hard times arouse an instinctive desire for authenticity' and it was

'I chose diamonds because they hold the greatest value within the smallest volume.'

important to 'invest'.[3] Another reason – and this explanation is more in tune with her passionate character – is that she had met a man who was to become her partner both in work and in love. Paul Iribe was an artist and cartoonist already noted for his fashion and jewelry designs. He had even designed some fabrics for Chanel. Like Coco herself, he was exuberant by nature, strong-minded and

charismatic. In his company, Mademoiselle expressed her attraction for the stars, her love for things that sparkle, her desire for a jewel that would resemble no other existing gem. He approved, shared her enthusiasm, and encouraged her quest for the absolute. The 'Bijoux de Diamants' that Coco Chanel designed were pure extravagance: a sumptuous use of stones, innovative motifs and forms, pieces that transformed, came apart and became something new.

Mademoiselle drew her inspiration from the heavens and the world of couture, an source of inspiration that allowed her to realize her wildest dreams. Stars of all sizes, galaxies, comets, crescent moons, as well as ribbons, bows, fringes and feathers metamorphose into voluptuous, stunning, dazzling necklaces, diadems, brooches and headpieces. Coco Chanel never intended 'to compete with the jewellers', or so she claimed. She simply wanted to 'give a new lease of life to a very French artform'.[4] Sometimes the jewelry seemed raw and unfinished; it shook people's expectations and let their imaginations run wild. Mademoiselle wanted her creations to embrace women and mould to their movements; just like her clothes, they had to be flexible, mobile and versatile.

Today, the famous 'Comète' necklace – the centrepiece of Chanel Fine Jewelry – has been

Previous pages
'Swing' necklace in 18-carat white gold with 955 diamonds for a total weight of 46.5 carats including a 7.5-carat oval brilliant-cut diamond, mounted on flexible 18-carat white gold threads.

Opposite
1932 'Étoile' brooch in platinum and old cut diamonds. In the centre, a 1.5-carat diamond raised on 5 claws in a surround of 19 bezel-set diamonds. Each of the five branches ends with 10 mounted diamonds.

reissued. It drapes round the neck with no clasp, no setting that is visible. Mademoiselle wanted women to be playful with their jewels, to display them in all their glory for special occasions and take them apart for day wear, using them as brooches or pendants or to adorn their hats or furs: 'Jewelry is not unchanging. Life transforms it and makes it bend to its requirements.'[5]

But what did jewelry represent for Coco Chanel? Perhaps it was primarily a question of feeling, a fairytale, an (im)moral fable whose one true value was love. For her, love was the most precious of possessions, and one that could not be measured in carats. Her jewelry designs were influenced by her personal life, her circle of friends, her encounters. It cannot be denied that she had a true passion for jewels. Throughout her life, she was never seen without them. She wore them every day, combining them with a sense of luxury, style and innovation. In every picture of her, she is seen wearing jewelry: some that she herself designed, some given to her by the men in her life, which she was always careful to combine with costume jewelry, as if to instantly erase any trace of what she called 'arrogance'. She also loved to lend her jewelry as easily as she would a scarf or a pair of stockings.

One of the first jewels to make her truly happy – or at least the first one that counts (she gave Étienne Balsan all his jewelry back after they had separated, except for one topaz) – was a present from Boy Capel. 'I never give you any presents', he once declared. The very next day, Gabrielle Chanel

received a tiara in its case. 'Should I wear it around my neck?' she asked. 'It's for the Opera,'[6] he replied. Perhaps she would have preferred to receive a bouquet of flowers from her elegant boyfriend Boy, as she went on to suggest. The next day, a bouquet of flowers arrived… half an hour later another one… and yet another. Boy Capel wanted to 'teach her happiness', she told Paul Morand. At that time, she was in love and still blissfully happy. Shortly afterwards, the Duke of Westminster, the richest man in England, perhaps in Europe, showered her with gifts. Westminster enjoyed her company because she was French and lively. But Gabrielle became utterly bored with the 'idle life of the rich'[7] and so she left. She always knew when to leave. During their liaison, she threw a

Above
'Comète' ring in platinum and diamond, a reissue of the 1932 design, finished with a 1-carat diamond.

Opposite
'Éléments Célestes 04' necklace. A cosmic explosion, 11 planets in a whirl of pearls, sapphires and diamonds bursting with magical energy. 2006 diamonds (33 carats), 404 sapphires (5.10 carats), 3 South Sea pearls measuring about 13 mm each and 2 faceted rock crystal balls give this necklace a cosmic feel.

Opposite

Above, the 'Soleil' brooch
in platinum set with
407 diamonds (total
17 carats). Inspired by an
ancient Ottoman motif, its
rays of varying lengths are
set with 406 diamonds, and
stream out from a central
diamond of more than
3 carats. Below it, the
'Deux Étoiles' piece is
18-carat white gold, set
with 461 diamonds (total
weight 55.13 carats).
Photo Karl Lagerfeld.

Right

'Nuit Étoilée' necklace
in 18-carat white gold
set with 316 sapphires
(261 carats) and
251 diamonds (20 carats).

The Chanel N° 5 necklace. The Fine Jewelry ateliers worked in secret and feverish excitement for four weeks on this piece, specially designed for Nicole Kidman. As the ambassadress of N° 5, the star wears it in Baz Luhrmann's extraordinary commercial. The necklace is one metre long and made from 18-carat white gold; it comprises 320 diamonds totalling 13 carats. The hero of this sumptuous and magical adventure, the N° 5 necklace will not be sold but will enter the archives of Chanel Fine Jewelry.

magnificent emerald he had given her into the sea out of frustration after a quarrel, because she still believed that a precious stone's only value was that of passion. She had been betrayed – so her emerald was no longer worth anything.

It was Grand Duke Dmitri, grandchild of Tsar Alexander II and first cousin of Nicolas II, who introduced her to opulence. This Russian magnificence was a far cry from British discretion. Dmitri presented her with a gold necklace composed of long irregular

'Why does all I do become Byzantine?'

chains, which she wore on many occasions, in combination with her beloved pearls and a little costume jewelry. But above all, her Russian lover taught her Slav luxury and baroque sumptuousness, which soon began to influence her designs.

Even back in the twenties, Chanel, the queen of the 'little black dress', had shown a taste for bold, theatrical jewelry. That is why she chose to surround herself with creators who, as always, were also her admirers. She was only ever drawn to people who were different,

those who, like her friend Misia Sert, shared her imagination, her culture, her passion for travel. One evening, before the diamond exhibition, she met the Palermo-born duke Fulco di Verdura, at a gala in Venice. She soon suggested he come to work for her. They had a lot in common, including the rejection of anything that resembled traditional jewelry in any way. Above all, they loathed the very popular 'solitaire' rings: they were too obvious, too banal. Fulco di Verdura worked with Coco Chanel to reinvent ancient forms, drawing inspiration from the motif of the Maltese cross – a motif Chanel would always favour – and designing dazzling bracelets studded with brilliant, boldly coloured baroque stones. Jewels evocative of ancient Greece or Byzantium; huge, barbarian jewels that were the epitome of the Chanel style both in size and in the choice of materials. As early as 1924, Chanel entrusted the creation of these jewels to one of the greatest Paris ateliers in that field, the Maison Gripoix. Their expertise in poured glass was unparalleled, and they gave pearls an incomparable golden sheen.

Mademoiselle's designs were influenced by the Louvre, her trips to Vienna and Munich, and above all, the Treasury of St Mark's in Venice, which she first visited in the company of Grand Duke Dmitri and later with her 'dear Misia'. In jewelry, she constantly sought

Opposite
'Mosaïque' gold bangle that once belonged to Coco Chanel, encrusted with baguette-cut rubies and sapphires, 1930s.

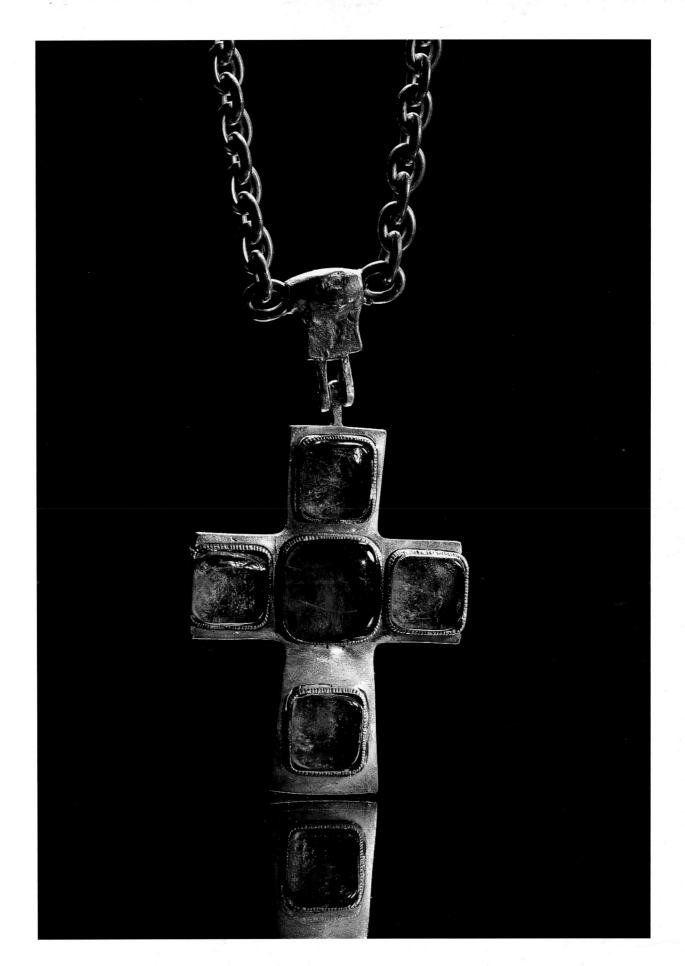

Opposite
Maltese cross brooches
in 18-carat yellow gold,
decorated with semi-
precious cabochons: citrine,
tourmaline, peridot, topaz.
A Fulco di Verdura design
from the 1930s. These
brooches belonged to the
legendary Diana Vreeland,
former editor of US *Vogue*.

Right
Bronze pendant cross set
with red and green glass,
dangling from a heavy bail.
Designed by Robert
Goossens for the 1971
Spring–Summer Haute
Couture collection.

historical arts and crafts that would open up a world of dreams. The most sumptuous of jewels had to begin as an idea, an ornament, and always an exclusive creation. Advice from socialites such as Étienne de Beaumont and her friendship with great writers and artists ranging from Jean Cocteau to Christian Bérard, through to Stravinsky and Picasso, had given her a different vision of fashion, art, history and the contemporary world, and played a crucial role in determining her personal perception of jewelry. Just as she was wont to do with her clothes, Chanel readily wore her own jewelry designs, especially the 'Venetian-style' ring and cuff bracelets that she was particularly fond of. The emerald cabochons, the sapphires and the rubies of majestic proportions mounted on matte gold would have taken anyone's breath away! More than anything, she loved their strength, their contrasts, the way they highlighted the simplicity of a suit or the demanding elegance of black. With the panache of a stylist, she wore jewelry at any time, night or day, and displayed its exuberance with unabashed daring. Sometimes she dismantled and reinvented it – its intrinsic qualities of beauty and love were the only things that mattered.

It would be impossible to talk about Coco Chanel without paying homage to pearls. They were as much an integral part of her

style and image as her little black dresses. They embodied her timeless elegance, her cultivation of beauty; they were an expression of her femininity. Only pearls could highlight dark tanned skin, only pearls could bring out sparkling eyes and white

'Go and fetch my pearls. I will not go up to the ateliers until I have them around my neck.'

teeth. Only pearls could capture the light, illuminate the face, embellish it like an invisible layer of makeup. Some say Coco Chanel's taste for pearls dated back to her liaison with Boy Capel, others to the gifts from Grand Duke Dmitri. Still others claim she was always fond of the oriental pearls in Renaissance paintings. The mystery remains.

When Chanel made her comeback in 1954, Paris remembered her first and foremost for her chunky costume jewelry. These pieces were part of the house vocabulary, a key feature of the celebrated Chanel look that the most fashionable women aspired to. Now that fashion had been democratized, luxury

Opposite
Coco Chanel: a 20th-century legend in her apartment at the Ritz in 1937. Photo François Kollar.

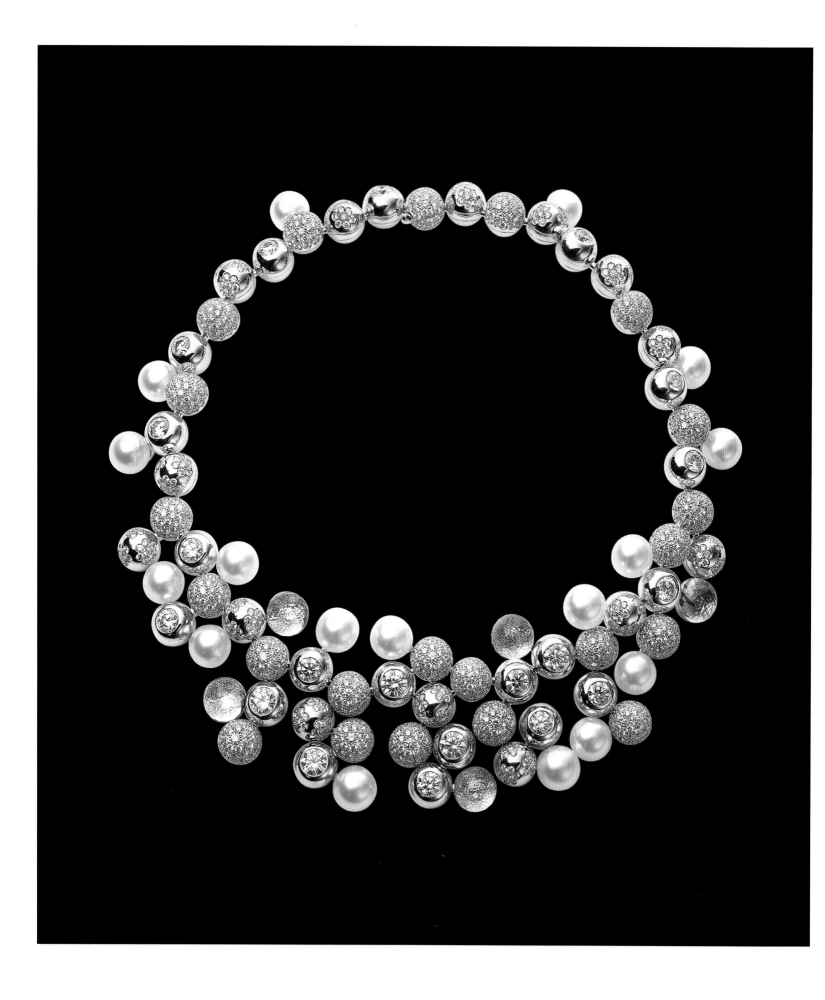

Opposite

'Eléments Célestes 02'
necklace, including 1,377
diamonds, 17 cultured
pearls measuring around
10 mm each and 5
hemispheres of faceted rock
crystal. Made from moving
spheres, this sumptuously
elegant necklace can be
easily reshaped and
transformed, recalling the
motion of the planets.

Right

'Volute' necklace in white
gold, pavé set with
diamonds. Alternating
South Sea pearls and
25 pear-cut diamonds
ranging from 1 to 6 carats
for a total of 145 carats,
it took fourteen months to
make. This necklace was
designed to be the star and
centrepiece of the Chanel
Fine Jewelry collection,
first launched in 1993.

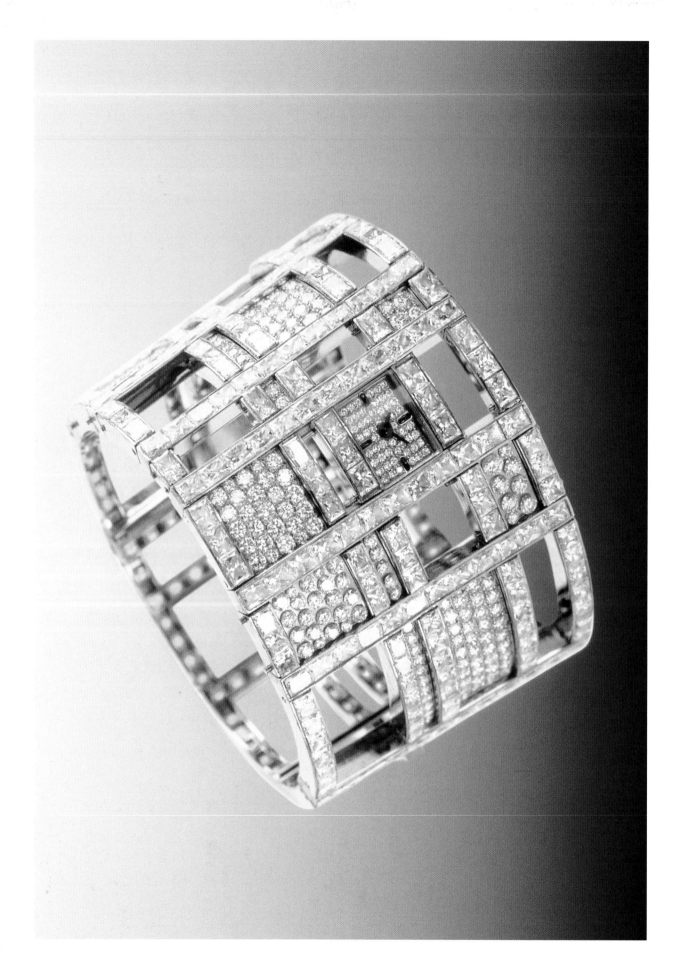

Left
'Cosmos' cuff watch in
18-carat white gold and
diamonds. Its ergonomic
lines allow the bracelet to
hug the arm perfectly. It
is structured around an
articulated framework
of white gold, set with
365 brilliant-cut diamonds.

Opposite
Actress Carole Bouquet
wears the 'Fontaine'
necklace, a reissue of the
1932 original in platinum,
adorned with 405
diamonds. A strand of
diamonds falls from the
base of the throat,
decorated with two
diamond-studded tassels
that recall fountains.

jewels were no longer de rigueur. The age of accessories had begun.

Only Robert Goossens continued to create the fine jewelry so dear to Mademoiselle for her collections, using the same precious materials he used in the twenties and thirties. The Goossens atelier has now joined the five other specialized craft workshops under the Chanel subsidiary, Paraffection, and this outstanding master goldsmith continues to make his exclusively handcrafted rock crystal, enamel, wood or metal creations. His magic touch brings all the materials to life, infusing them with a timeless, seductive charm.

A resurgence or a diversification? In 1987, the Chanel House inaugurated a Watch boutique and opened a Fine Jewelry department. The face of the first watch created by Jacques Helleu, grandson of the painter Paul Helleu, recalls the stopper of the N° 5 bottle. Its octagonal shape mounted with diamonds makes it unique. Then a series of jewelled watches with feminine lines was created. Chanel's artistic director went on to invent the bestselling J12, a sports watch in black ceramic, later interpreted in white. The designer apparently dreamed up the watch based on a personal whim, faithful to the way that Mademoiselle herself used to work. The first jewelry to bear the Chanel logo was in fact all based on her personal tastes. Gold and diamonds sparkling in the hazy sun of the Normandy beaches; this collection owed its inspiration to the world

of the sea: precious shells, shell-motif rings harbouring invisible pearls, other rings that coil around the finger; pin brooches too, and clip brooches reminiscent of Mademoiselle's first hats; or large cuff bracelets in matte gold to be worn as a talisman in true Mademoiselle style. Simple jewels for everyday wear, suitable for city or beach.

A short time later came the grand première. On 18 November 1997, at 18 place Vendôme, opposite the Ritz to be precise, Chanel opened its first Fine Jewelry boutique. A sumptuous jewel-box setting in an *hôtel particulier* with Chinese screens, warm golden panelling, shining mirrors, easy chairs and beige carpeting: the stage was well and truly set to receive the new creations. The spirit of 1932 was reborn: comet necklaces, shooting stars, fringes and ribbons, with diamonds as the star attraction, just like in the days of Coco herself. She is said to have spent many an evening taking her own jewels out of their settings and then remounting them in wax and modelling clay, as her fancy took her. The jewels in this treasure trove are marvels of imagination, refinement and craftsmanship. Their unique ergonomic mechanisms allow them to be taken apart.

Opposite
'Planète' necklace in
18-carat yellow gold, with
555 coloured diamonds
(total weight 70 carats)
and 47 coloured pearls.
Chanel Fine Jewelry.

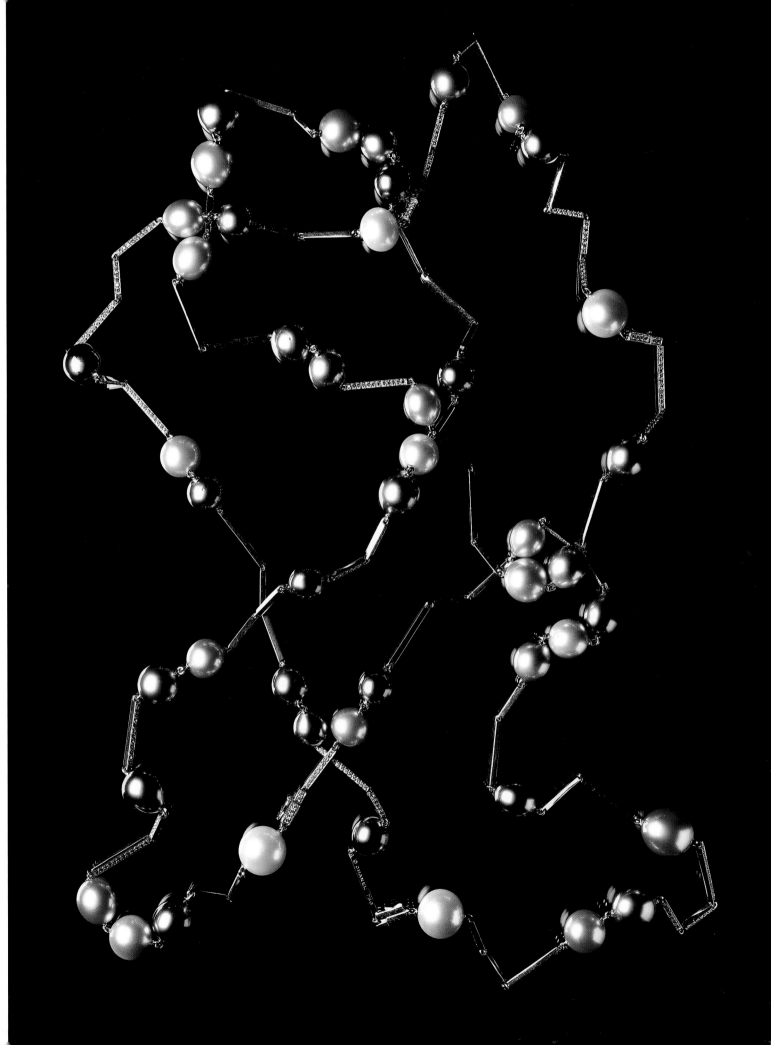

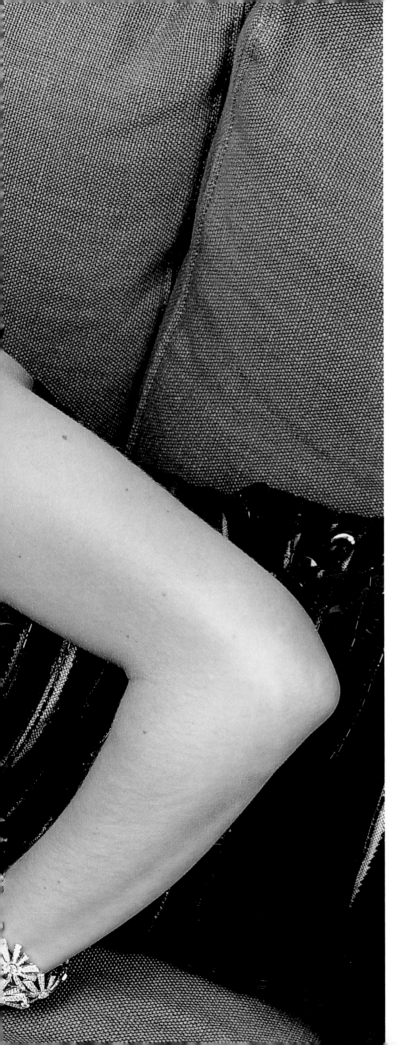

Worn here by Anna
Mouglalis, the 'Sphères'
sautoir is made from
multicoloured South Sea
and Tahitian pearls
interspersed with 8
18-carat gold beads set
with green, brown and
yellow diamonds. This
necklace can be also
converted into a choker
and two bracelets.
The 'Planète' necklace
comprises 3 separate
strands in 18-carat white
gold set with white
diamonds, interspersed with
large grey, white and gold
South Sea pearls. The
'Soleil' bracelet in platinum,
is composed of 1,016
diamonds, with a total
weight of 25 carats.
Photo Lee Jenkins.

According to Chanel spokespeople, their only development strategy is to respect the house image, and to nourish and enrich it by designing Fine Jewelry that bears comparison with the house's couture lines. What counts are quality, precision and novelty. In 1998 for instance, *Les Fables Impertinentes de Chanel* (Chanel's Impertinent Fables) teamed gold

'Some of my necklaces do not close, but follow the line of the neck; some of my rings coil up.'

with diamonds, pearls with gemstones for a collection of animal motifs that combined the house icons with a touch of humour and boundless imagination. Some pearl and gemstone necklaces as intricate as embroidery were seen for the first time. In 1999, the *Passage* collection confirmed the house passion for innovation, the magnetism of the planets and the music of the spheres. There was a galaxy of pearls; 'Météorite' or 'Équinoxe' necklaces; 'Cosmos' watches that fit the arm perfectly.

Every year or so, drawing on a tradition dear to Coco Chanel, a contemporary artist is chosen to stage a presentation of these jewels. In 2001, Jean-Paul Goude presented the *Cinq Éléments* (Five Elements), underscoring the intimate relationship between the world of Chanel and the world of symbols. 'It's the theatrical aspect of jewelry that fascinates me', Coco Chanel once declared upon returning from a trip to Russia, where she had seen Ivan the Terrible's crown jewels at the Kremlin. In 2002, Ingo Maurer presented the reissued *Bijoux de Diamants* collection; the 'Comète 2002' necklace with 3,590 diamonds, the 'Fontaine' necklace, the 'Franges' necklace and the 'Poussières d'Étoiles' range, recalling the delicate lacework used in the couture lines, to celebrate the seventieth anniversary of the first showing of this famous collection. In the Collections Privées, magnificence vies with ingenuity: one of the most spectacular necklaces, 'Volute', features a double row of pear-cut diamonds and pearls, and took more than a thousand hours to make! In 2003, the *Cristaux Glacés* (Ice Crystals) gave a new geometricity to jewelry design, recalling blocks of ice swept along by the Neva river or sparkling frost clinging to palace windows, as Grand Duke Dmitri might have described to Mademoiselle. Icy fragments of quartz, their inclusions set with precious stones, and necklaces and rings studded with diamonds recall the sublime, crystalline transparency of frozen water.

Opposite
Portrait of Coco Chanel wearing multiple strings of pearls. Photo Boris Lipnitzki, October 1936.

'I want jewels to be like ribbons in a woman's hands. My ribbons are supple and flexible.'

A pendant in the shape of a comet, a necklace like a starry cloud of shining spheres, heavenly rings made of rare gems: 'these jewels must speak for themselves', insists the director of Fine Jewelry. With the exception of the camellia, few of the house emblems are reproduced in jewelry. Each piece does, however, send out a message of love or of modernity. The colour of each stone is a reflection of style: the ethereal, starry white of the diamond, the oriental lustre of the pearl, the blue of the sapphire.

The 2003 Collection Privée was a journey to the heart of Chanel via the key themes of her creative universe, recalled by the names of the pieces: 'Icône Camélia', 'Inspiration Byzantine', 'Perles', 'Allure'. In 2004, the Collection Privée celebrated the colours of Mademoiselle's favourite stones with a line of creations bursting with imagination and luxury. Tourmalines in pink, pearls in dusky rose, diamonds in a palette ranging from the palest of pinks through to lilac and even fuchsia. The classic diamond reinterpreted the themes of the 1932 collection, namely stars and comets; the sapphire evoked the journey from night to day; the ruby, a symbol of wild romance, recalled Mademoiselle's passionate temperament; the emeralds conjured memories of the ones that the Duke of Westminster gave to Coco Chanel; the pearls recalled those that were once Mademoiselle's own talisman.

In the spring of 2005, it was the turn of the artist Xavier Veilhan to be invited to envision an innovative world based around the sixteen 'Éléments Célestes', a collection studded with more than 15,000 diamonds, sapphires and pearls. The exhibition took the form of a journey of exploration to another planet, a 'dream machine' that revealed a universe alive with moving spheres and cosmic motion, an imaginative landscape that showcased the timelessness of the Chanel style and the way that its dazzling creativity will send it sailing into the future.

Opposite
Anna Mougalis wears 'Camélias Aquatiques' rings in 18-carat white gold and semi-precious stones.
Photo Patrick Demarchelier

FRAGRANCE & BEAUTY

'To be irreplaceable, one must be different.'

'Two long black despotic eyebrows'[1], dark eyes, a pale and powdered complexion, an intensely red mouth never without lipstick: Coco Chanel's beauty expressed demanding perfectionism, which she cultivated to her dying day. Her makeup reflected her personality like an identity card, with her 'distinguishing features' inscribed on her face like calligraphic strokes denoting, in the words of Paul Morand, 'bluntness and a dexterous precision'. They reveal a powerful femininity, which made no concessions to the longstanding image of womanhood that she rejected. She soon invented a style of her own to which she remained faithful to the end – pitch-black hair, which she cut herself one morning in 1917; a thick fringe, which accentuated her

dark eyes – she would later impose the same fringe on her house models – onyx eyes enhanced by dark eye makeup and 'impatient'[2] lips highlighted with bright red lipstick. Mademoiselle's bag always contained several compacts so she could touch up her makeup at any time to ensure it reflected her impeccable image or to intensify it for evening wear. Constantly on the lookout for modern, practical yet elegant solutions, she perfected everyday fashion and beauty products to meet her personal needs and desires, and the fierce demands she placed on her appearance. She was a severe self-critic: 'I can see my menacing double-arched eyebrows…the harshness in the mirror reflects my own harshness.'[3] She never once wavered from her self-imposed discipline, never accepted any excuses, and never tolerated laziness.

Mademoiselle was never seen bare-faced and wore vermilion red on her lips at all times, retouching automatically as soon as the colour began to fade. So in 1921 – needs must when 'Mademoiselle' drives – she made herself the first 'stick' of blood-red lip colour, simply protected in a tube of waxed paper: she had created the precursor to today's ready-to-wear lipstick. Before long, Mademoiselle, who loved this feminine ritual, improved the presentation by creating

Previous pages
This exclusive logo brush is made of 16,000 silk strands and entirely hand-crafted. Designed 2005. Photo Didier Roy.

Opposite
Portrait of Gabrielle Chanel by Hoyningen-Huene, 1935.

for herself a very delicate mother-of-pearl tube, then a push-up case in gunmetal grey which she soon marketed. At first Coco Chanel had it stamped with a single C, then in 1930 came the mythical CC, the architecturally perfect monogram, which continues to symbolize the Chanel style. For Coco Chanel, lipstick was so essential that she even included a special pocket for it in her quilted handbag – soon to become famous as the legendary 2-55 – so as to always have it at hand. She regarded lipstick as the ultimate weapon of seduction. She loved deep red, which flattered her dark hair and 'golden brown' eyes; it added a dash of elegance, that crucial touch of sophistication. In 1974, an exact copy of Mademoiselle's favourite shade of lipstick was made under the name of 'Rouge de Chanel'.

Every season, Dominique Moncourtois and Heidi Morawetz, Chanel's two makeup creators, give lipsticks a starring role, as befits their bestselling status. They develop eight new shades for each collection while constantly seeking to improve texture and colour intensity. Today, Chanel lipstick is still able to produce effects that can surprise and delight even long-time aficionados. Gloss, shine and special light-reflecting colours have created a new age, an age in which anything is possible! Hydrating lipsticks and easy-to-wear textures have been around for a

long time but are becoming lighter and lighter while continuing to provide perfect coverage. Rouge Hydrabase, created in 1968, carries on being a top product thanks to its perfect balance between hold, radiance, softness and suppleness. The innovative Infra Rouge provides consistent depth and luminosity in all lighting conditions. Aqualumière ensures comfort and sheer

'Beauty is not prettiness. Why do so many mothers teach their daughters to flutter about, instead of teaching them about beauty?'

colour while gently protecting the lips. From pale beige to deep plum, more than fifteen shades shape the lips' sensual curves. As for lipglosses, the latest Lèvres Scintillantes Glossimer range adds sparkle and shine.

Coco Chanel had a natural instinct for beauty. She believed a specific product

CRÈME
CHANEL
POUR PEAUX SÈCHES

CHANEL
PARIS

CHANEL
PARIS

CHANEL
PARIS

CRÈME
DE
MAQUILLAGE

CRÈME
DE
JOUR
POUR PEAUX SÈCHES

CRÈME
DE
NETTOYAGE

Above

A futuristic vision of beauty on the move: small, easy-to-carry tubes of cream created in 1948, available for all types of skin.

Opposite

Above, a skin astringent created in 1930. Below, face cream from 1929. Well ahead of her time, Coco Chanel wanted all her beauty products to be available in a travel size.

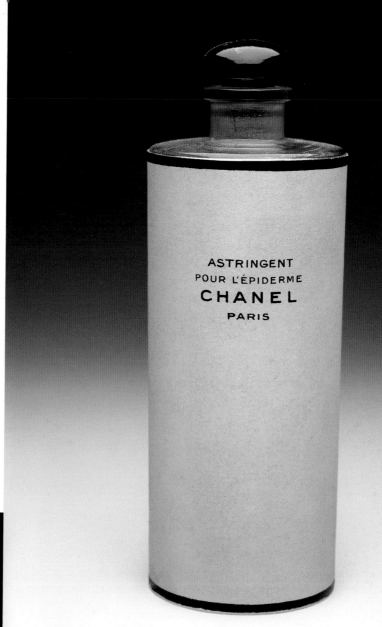

Above
Perfumed talcum powder was introduced in around 1930, packaged in a container with simple lines that Mademoiselle was particularly fond of.

Left
One of Coco Chanel's favourite pastimes was sunbathing. Huile Tan was created in 1926 and reformulated in 1947, while Poudre Tan was created in 1934, updated in 1950.

Opposite
Pure, rich, nourishing jasmine oil, recommended by Mademoiselle for facial massages.

should correspond to a specific need. Here again, her own requirements influenced her creations. She took care of her skin and removed her makeup every evening, so in 1927, she developed astringent-soaked makeup-remover wipes. Only a perfect, flawless matte complexion was acceptable, one that would never let her down. She also had the discreet habit of keeping a little fine powder in a white lawn handkerchief hidden up her jacket sleeve. With her usual visionary acumen, she soon created a packet of powdered papers to remove shine, an idea which the Japanese, lovers of pale, pure complexions, would take up sixty years later.

What was Coco's Chanel idea of beauty? A firm, fairly thin but athletic body – sports represented discipline and inner strength, virtues she not only lauded but also expected of herself. At a time when the criteria of perfection was pale, fair skin as portrayed in early women's magazines, Chanel transgressed tradition – dark and sensual, with a 'Bohemian complexion' that brought out the 'dual whiteness'[4] of her teeth and her pearls. She loved the sea and the sun, exposed her arms and neckline and dared to sport a tan. But she instinctively sensed the need to protect her skin from sunburn, so in 1924, she invented Huile Tan, the first sun-tan oil. She would later ask her researchers to work on UV filters to add to her oil. Shortly afterwards, she extended her range of 'sun-kissed' makeup with Poudre Tan, similar to the bronzing powders used today.

Coco Chanel also had the audacity to wear trousers and sailor tops, or to sport a

'Beauty should begin in the heart and soul, otherwise cosmetics are useless.'

bathing costume. Her 'too thin' body, 'as dry as a vine with no grapes',[5] suited her. She liked this 'flatness in the body', ignored its attributes – breasts, hips – which did not correspond to her conception of femininity, and instead favoured ease of movement, posture, and above all, allure. She advocated an 'honest' diet, a 'simple but moderate' appetite, enough sleep. 'Nothing amuses me after midnight', she declared in an interview with Djuna Barnes in September 1931. Long before health specialists the world over, she sensed the importance of what is now

Opposite
Marie-Hélène Arnaud, Mimi d'Arcangues and Paule Rizzo at a makeup session back in the days of Coco.

Opposite
From the first push-up
lipstick created by Gabrielle
Chanel for personal use in
1924 to the famous Rouge
Hydrabase lipstick launched
in 1968, Mademoiselle's
favourite red has grown into
a wide palette of colours.
Coco Chanel always started
from the same base and
simply created variations on
the theme from year to year.

'Since it is agreed that the eyes reflect the soul, why not admit that the mouth reveals the heart?'

Opposite
Ad for Rouge Extrême
Chanel, an 'intense,
lasting and provocative'
lipstick. Photo Daniel
Jouanneau, 1982.

dubbed 'healthy living', to which she added her own philosophy, her life-long guiding principle: 'work, hard work' because a busy mind helps the body to stay lively. We should be loved for ourselves, for what we are, for what we do with ourselves. Time, she believed, is not the enemy of beauty as long as every woman learns to discover and shape her face over the years. Looks are indicative of a way of being. A youthful, slim silhouette like her own, a free and lively step, and a natural, supple body. She wanted to teach this very personal beauty strategy to all women, for very few – so she believed – knew how to 'transfer physical beauty to the mind', or accepted losing the 'prettiness of youth'[6] and replacing it with elegance of the soul.

Coco Chanel wanted to pass on her own unique approach, her talent for being different. She quickly learned to communicate the art and craft of makeup, the secret of illuminating the face without masking it. 'I don't understand how a woman can leave the house without fixing herself up a little – if only out of politeness. How pretentious to go out like that, bare-faced. You never know, maybe that's the day you have a date with destiny. And it's best to be as pretty as possible for destiny.'[7]

Mademoiselle wanted her first beauty products, powders and lipsticks to be instantly recognizable and carry the Chanel colours, or rather, her own favourite colour: exclusive, innovative black. In 1932, she heard about a remarkable new substance used in the automotive industry, called Bakelite. She immediately had the packaging for her makeup and portable products designed in that groundbreaking material. Today, the world over, these little black Bakelite cases – the material was later improved to make its surface stronger – still open up to reveal the glowing colours of Chanel cosmetics.

The year is 1969. Mademoiselle is examining the work of a young makeup artist on the face of one of the girls from the Chanel *cabine*, under the glare of the spotlights needed to create the strong light and shadow effects so beloved by Coco Chanel, inspired by the movies of the 1930s. Now, she nods in approval – a pale but radiant complexion, smoky eyes and bright red lips are exactly what she is looking for, the same look she has chosen for herself. This session was, in a manner of speaking, an entrance exam for Dominique Moncourtois who after that day rose to become Chanel's international director of makeup. 'I was fascinated by the vitality of this woman', he explains, 'who sculpted clothes around the models, commenting all the while on what she was doing, who pulled on a sleeve, tore it off, put it back in place, systematically trying on everything she created.' He watched and listened. 'A jacket', she declared, 'must always hang perfectly. A facelift should restructure a face without being noticeable. Perfection should be found where it is least suspected.'

Message understood! Dominique Moncourtois and Heidi Morawetz, who joined him in 1980, the two creators of the makeup collections, strive constantly to bring out the skin's luminosity from within. Since 1982, new pigment technology has literally transfigured the concept of glow and shine in makeup by creating light- and colour-reflecting effects. Every season, the creators reinvent the face of the 'Chanel woman' by reworking the house codes and colours. Building on the established Chanel 'family' of products, they design the makeup of tomorrow with a freedom that only the power of the Chanel brand can give them. Because time is on their side, no product leaves the design studio until it has been completely perfected. Their aims are often surprising and innovation is a constant. Moncourtois and Morawetz plan the collections five years ahead. Their only

'I take refuge in beige because it is natural, and in red because it is the colour of blood.'

demands are chic, surprise – in the spirit of the famous slogan 'Let Chanel surprise you' – and a desire to discover ways of making women's lives easier while enhancing their natural beauty.

Is there such a thing as a Chanel palette? Yes, given that black, white and beige, the house colours, provide the foundation for this creative drive and imagination. It is also true that the creators draw their inspiration for new variations not only from fashion trends but also from the history of the brand. Firm believers that anything is possible, they imagine sumptuous blues as precious as

Opposite
Chanel's Blanc Universel makeup base was revolutionary when it was launched in 1982. It is still a bestseller.

Overleaf
Luminosity, intensity, mystery and shine are the keywords for these stunning colour effects.

POUDRE UNIVERSELLE LIBRE
POUDRE LIBRE FINI NATUREL
NATURAL FINISH LOOSE POWDER

CHANEL

BRONZE UNIVERSEL DE CHANEL

CHANEL

BLANC UNIVERSEL DE CHANEL

CHANEL

TEINT COMPACT CRÈME UNIVERSEL
SPF 15

CHANEL

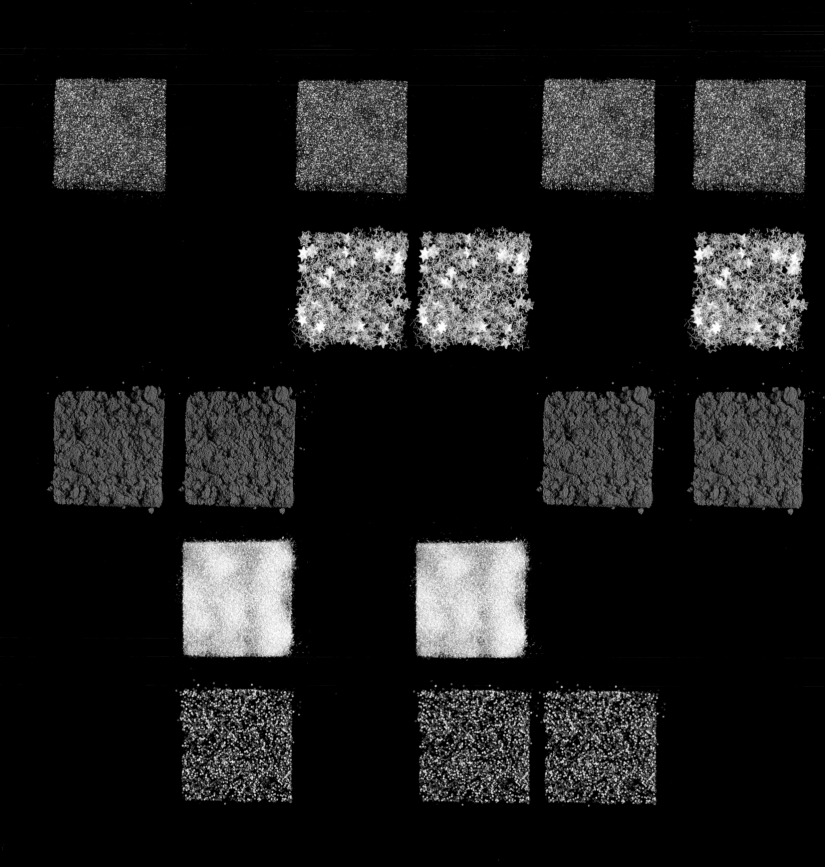

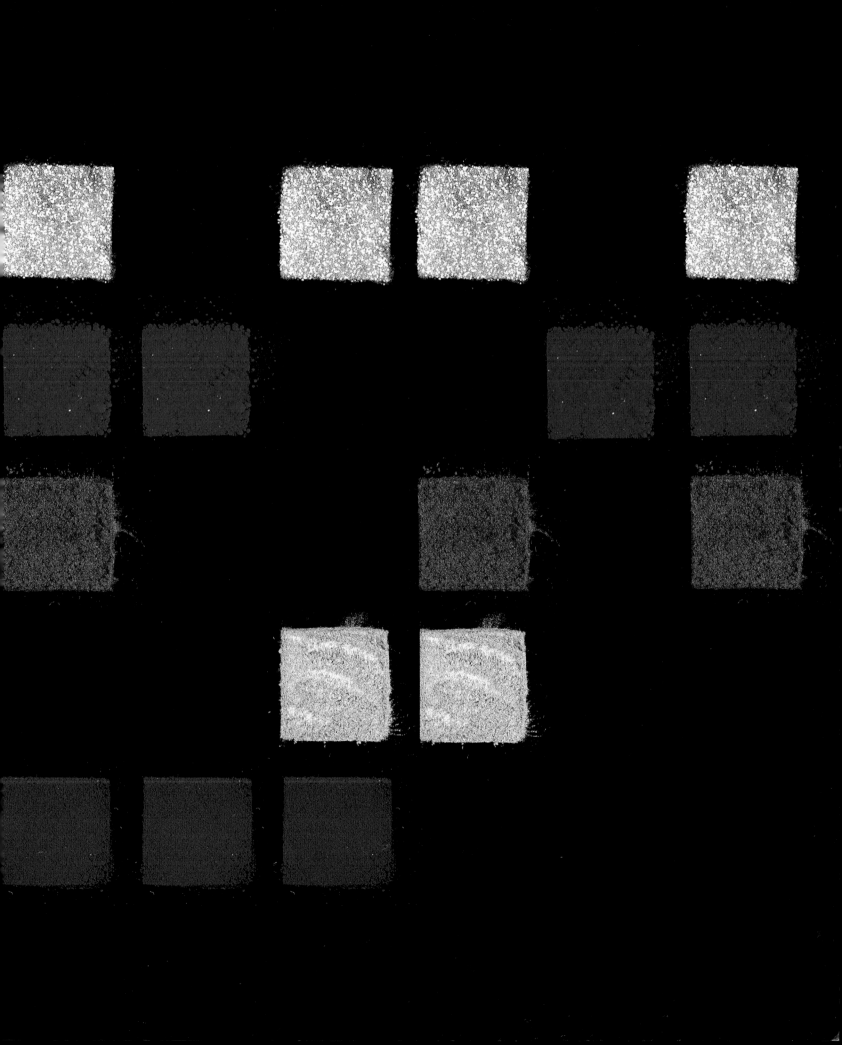

sapphires, lapis lazuli and turquoise, greens that conjure images of English lawns and misty landscapes, yellows like opal, honey and amber. In Spring 2005, they moved to a palatial new glass building where the natural light is ideal for creating colours and working on polychrome pigments.

For the past ten years, Chanel has been building its makeup collection around what were initially called the Éditions Éphémères, later dubbed the Star Products and, as of 2006, Créations Exclusives. The idea of these limited-edition products came into being above all to pay homage to the house legacy and as a result of the trailblazing success of 'L'Or de Chanel'. Created in 1995, this product was an almost exact replica of the first makeup to incorporate gold, invented by Mademoiselle in 1934. Drawing on the house culture, each new Création Exclusive determines the style, colours and textures for the forthcoming makeup collection. The creators get their inspiration to create surprising cosmetics from fashion – fabrics and jewelry are reimagined as irresistible jewel-like eyeshadows and blushers – and even from items in Mademoiselle's own home. Take for instance the Coromandels eyeshadow, created for the 2005 Autumn–Winter line, which was directly influenced by one of her Chinese lacquered screens. Or the Ruban Perlé compact created for Spring 2005, a reference to the ribbons she used to decorate her dresses and hair: a flurry of delicate pinks with an iridescent pearly sheen for eyes, cheeks or lips, evoking shantung, moiré or organdie silk.

'It is not really ideas that are important to us – currently, we have more than sixty projects on the drawing board – it's more the development of each product', the creators explain. 'Each product is a technological feat.' Thus it took more than fifteen years to shape the Perles de Chanel, the Star Product for Winter 2002, which contained the highest possible concentration of high-tech pigments in a single black compact. The quilted motif of Irréelle, a powder blush inspired by the iconic Chanel quilted bag, was the result of years of patient research: 'One day, we came across a technique used by a Brussels chocolate-maker which we used to isolate each square.' For Jeans, a pressed powder eyeshadow designed to

Previous pages, left
Each new Chanel foundation is based on the latest light pigment technology discovered in 1980 and constantly updated. The aim is to create glow, luminosity, and youthfulness.

Previous pages, right
Blusher pressed into the Chanel 'quilted' motif.

Above
From skin care to makeup, all Chanel beauty products bear the house logo.

Opposite
Mademoiselle's dressing table. Photo François Kollar, 1937.

Previous pages
The 'Créations Exclusives'
range, designed by
Dominique Moncourtois
and Heidi Morawetz from
1995 onwards. These
limited editions are all
boundlessly creative and
take their inspiration from
the brand heritage.

Opposite
Sequinned hand makeup for
the 2000 Spring–Summer
Haute Couture collection.
Photo Karl Lagerfeld.

Right
2001 ad campaign
for waterproof mascara.
Photos Ludes for Chanel.

151

imitate the texture and weave of denim with overstitching and fraying effects, Dominique Moncourtois and Heidi Morawetz combined five different technologies. A cutting-edge laser technique produced the denim-like speckled effect, then the surface was sprayed with gold, silver and blue to reproduce the Chanel logo and golden overstitching, just as they would be used in couture. For Ruban Perlé, a metallic mould was designed, using a positive/negative pressing technique to reproduce the effect of interwoven ribbons and overstitching.

Women the world over wait in breathless anticipation for the launch of each new limited edition as they would for a true work of art. 'It's the advent of a new generation of pigments that has enabled us to improve the art of makeup. Technology has generated a palette of rare and sublime colours, which make it possible to play with an infinite number of shades and light-reflecting effects. Similar to the play of light produced by the silk and sequins Mademoiselle was so fond of, our polychrome powders offer a host of possibilities!'

A perfume of eternal femininity, glorified by the most beautiful women in the world, by legendary stars from Marilyn Monroe in 1954 to Catherine Deneuve in 1970 and Nicole Kidman in 2004, Chanel N° 5 is not simply the bestselling perfume in the world: it is an olfactory work of art launched on

Opposite
Vicky Hilbert as seen by Richard Avedon's camera: a leap into the future for a legendary fragrance.

'Of all the human senses, smell is the most perfect.'

5 May 1921 by the woman who selected it and was its embodiment for more than half a century. Chanel N° 5, the first 'modern perfume' or 'abstract fragrance', is ageless.

Why is this blockbuster so successful? It is difficult to say but there are two keywords that might justify this passion. The first and most important is 'mystery'. Jacques Polge, the house perfumer, translates this as abstraction. Indeed, one of the secrets of Chanel perfumes is that no single 'essence' should stand out. A perfume's *sillage* (aura), on the other hand, should remain unique and be instantly recognizable. More than eighty-three components go into the making of N° 5, a figure unheard of at a time when perfumes were generally limited to a simple combination of floral fragrances. Chanel N° 5 was immediately recognized as being

153

New Glamour in Your Life

No. 5 *
No. 22 *
GARDENIA
GLAMOUR *
CUIR DE RUSSIE [RUSSIA LEATHER]
* REG. U. S. PAT. OFF.

CHANEL INC.

'Jasmine. Nothing is more expensive than jasmine.'

'Well then! Add more. I want to make the most expensive perfume in the world.'[8]

Since then, the quality of the jasmine has been constantly controlled and is currently monitored by Jacques Polge. The principal ingredients of the fragrance – especially the

totally different. Jasmine and rose were incorporated but reinterpreted and reinforced by floral aldehydes, which surprised, even shocked the perfume industry and revolutionized the perception of fragrance. At that time, nobody had heard of these molecules, or flower esters, which gave the scent its intensity, its aura, its strength, and aroused a sensuality that women – perhaps without realizing it – had been longing for.

The second keyword is 'quality', that of its natural components, unchanged since it was created. Whereas today the *sillages* of some of the greatest perfumes of the century are often disappointing – they seem less enduring, less memorable – that of N° 5 remains sacrosanct, untouchable, like an abstract painting, a living treasure protected from change.

When it was invented, Mademoiselle was, as usual, extremely demanding. Ernest Beaux, its creator, presented several of his compositions but only one held her attention. The perfumer raised a few objections: 'There are more than eighty ingredients in that sample. It will be very expensive,' he announced.

'Ah! And what is its most expensive ingredient?' she asked.

'A perfume should hit you… It should be intense, and it is the most costly ingredients that make a perfume intense.'

famed jasmine from Grasse, in southern France – are cultivated in their original regions in gardens reserved for Chanel. Another surprising feature in its day was the N° 5 bottle, a minimalist container selected by Mademoiselle. All the most attractive fragrances of the period were sold in conspicuously feminine and sophisticated bottles, but Coco Chanel chose to launch her perfume in an all-purpose bottle to highlight

Previous pages
Chanel N° 5 lithographs
by Andy Warhol, 1964.

Opposite
Ad for Chanel N° 5. *Vogue*
US, 1 March 1940.

Catherine Deneuve for Chanel

CHANEL

Perfume in the classic bottle from 8.50 to 400., Eau de Chanel from 7.00 to 20.00, Eau de Cologne from 4.00 to 20.00, Spray Perfume and Spray Cologne each 6.00.

the one thing that mattered, the fragrance itself. Applying the same principle as in fashion, she wanted nothing to prejudice her enigmatic perfume! So she decided to choose a very simple bottle with Art Deco lines, which went on to play a crucial role in its success. It celebrated its own difference and placed its seal on the times, heralding a new generation of bottle designs. The challenge in the years that followed was how to adapt the bottle to changing tastes and shapes while staying as close as possible to the spirit of the original. Chanel's Artistic Director Jacques Helleu is now responsible for these decisions, as he is for all beauty product packaging. His task is to protect the image and style of the brand while updating and modernizing its forms.

How can a perfume's success be made to last forever? Perhaps, above all, by never attempting to recreate that fragrance. Almost all of the perfumes launched by Chanel over recent years are in the top ten bestseller list but not one of them has ever tried to imitate the classic fragrance in any way. The original N° 5 remains unique. Today it is called Extrait de Parfum to avoid any possible confusion. To update the scent, other concentrations are invented, extending the N° 5 range. Jacques Polge created the Eau de Toilette N° 5 with a note of sandalwood and Elixir Sensuel N° 5 with delicate floral notes providing silky freshness. A perfume's prosperity also relies on finding the perfect advertising strategy. The fragrance's international success was driven by a series of spectacular advertising campaigns geared to the United States. 'I was afraid young people would see N° 5 as a perfume for their mothers. In 1968, we had the idea of dressing a young model all in white. Shortly afterwards, by a perfect stroke of luck, I came across a picture of Chanel dressed in white trousers and a jacket when she was visiting her friends, the Bernsteins. I think it was predestined.' Jacques Helleu saved the first glamorous publicity drive for the US, with Catherine Deneuve who agreed to represent the fragrance's American image. Photographed by Richard Avedon, she personified beauty and refinement. Since then the greatest photographers and artists have portrayed Chanel perfumes. The Artistic Director gives them carte blanche to create an image that will convey a contemporary spirit.

'Surprising but not shocking' is Jacques Helleu's motto. 'We have often asked the most beautiful women in the world to be the ambassadresses of N° 5. Nicole Kidman, whom I thought looked divine in Baz Luhrmann's film *Moulin Rouge*, has been N° 5's new star since November 2004.' A star among stars, she moves through Luhrmann's promotional movie looking gorgeous, sensual and ephemeral. Just like the fragrance itself, whose intensity and mystery are only heightened with the passage of time….

Previous pages
Catherine Deneuve photographed by Richard Avedon for Chanel N° 5. Ad campaign used exclusively in the US from 1968 to 1977.

Opposite
International star Nicole Kidman, a new image for N° 5, as sketched by Karl Lagerfeld.

161

THE BLACK DRESS

'Dress women in black or white at a ball. They will catch the eye.'

In a move away from excessive lyricism and unnecessary clutter, Coco Chanel launched the 'little black dress' in the early twenties. It was 'little' because it was discreet yet essential, minimalist yet elegant, obvious yet sophisticated. A woman dressed in black draws attention to herself, not to her dress. 'Nothing is more difficult to make than a little black dress. The entrancing tricks of Scheherazade are much easier to copy,'[1] Mademoiselle Chanel declared, referring to the ostentatious designs of Paul Poiret, in one of her eminently quotable soundbites, a terse judgment that clearly condemned what she found 'distasteful'.

'The richer the dress, the poorer it becomes,' she explained, advocating a novel kind of 'austere luxury', a new fashion language that immediately became a landmark, the quintessence of chic.

Was the black dress truly a new design? Not exactly. Gabrielle Chanel's genius lay in her ability to reinvent an existing garment, to reinterpret and restyle it, to transport it to the dizzying heights of desirable fashion with the talent of an unrelenting pioneer. What actually inspired Chanel to create the dress remains somewhat of a mystery. Was it an expression of nostalgia? Did it recall her sad, neglected childhood? Did it remind her of that dark shapeless uniform she wore day in and day out at the orphanage in Aubazine, where she learned the meaning of solitude when she was only twelve? At that time, as she confided to Paul Morand, her only refuge was the 'little old country cemetery' where she felt like 'a queen in a secret garden'. Or did the idea come later, when she discovered the almost erotic strictness of the black dresses with white trimmings worn by chambermaids and household servants? Or perhaps her sole purpose was to highlight the strict beauty of the simplest shapes by subjecting them to her visionary fashion instinct? Other designers had worked on black dresses

Previous pages
The 'little black dress', 1920s style: an interpretation of the iconic dress over the decades by Karl Lagerfeld for *Vogue* US. Photo Karl Lagerfeld.

Opposite
Mademoiselle in her studio in the late sixties. As was her custom, garments were designed, modelled, fitted and constantly reworked on a live model. Photo Douglas Kirkland.

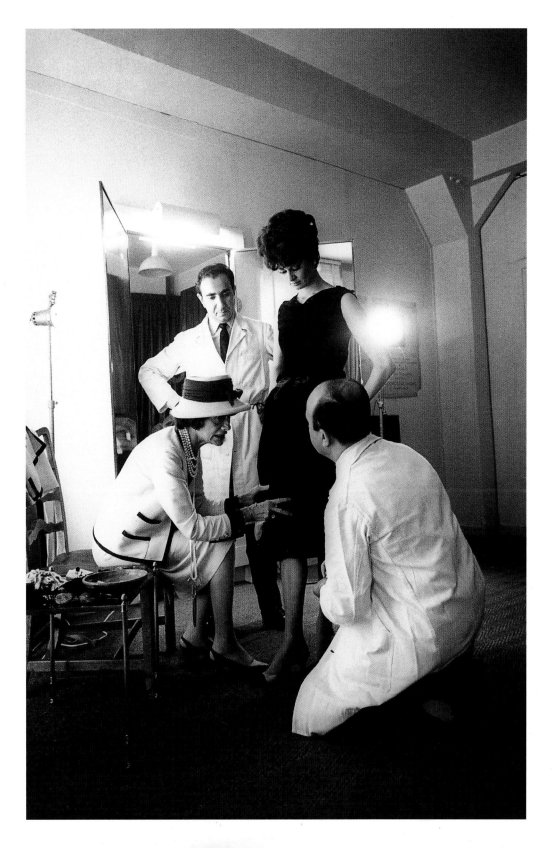

before her, but none had turned them into a concept, nor had they made them suitable for day wear, cocktail wear and evening wear as Chanel did.

In the 1920s, she decided – with her unequalled talent for juggling daring and paradox – to rid women's fashion of pointless frills and frou-frou. It is said that one evening at the opera, she was 'appalled by the resurgence of flashy, gaudy colours': 'All those electric reds, greens and blues, the entire palette of Rimsky-Korsakov and Gustave Moreau, brought back into fashion by Poiret sickened me. The Ballets Russes is for the stage, not for couture... Those colours are impossible. I'm going to put all those women in little black dresses.'[2] She rejected the use of ostentatious fabrics, preferring to use crêpe to create a simple sheath...in black, of course. A round neckline, long, close-fitting sleeves, a skirt just below the knees, lines that hugged the body. Pure and simple. No embroidery, no draped fabrics, no fringes, no sequins: nothing but simplicity at its purest.

The outcry was immediate. Detractors criticized the look of those 'underfed telegraph operators with no bust and no hips'. But Coco Chanel persisted: 'Better to choose to strip oneself than to be stripped by others.' The 'democratic' black dress was already being called 'the modern woman's uniform'. In November 1926, *Vogue* magazine dubbed it the 'Ford dress', alluding to the famous standardized car,

'A woman can be overdressed, never over-elegant.'

and just like its namesake automobile, the dress met with unprecedented success. In fact, for this design, later to become an icon of fashion history, Chanel had applied Ford's principles of radical simplicity. The crêpe de Chine 'Ford' dress – reused by Karl Lagerfeld in almost exactly the same form for the 1999–2000 Autumn–Winter Haute Couture Collection – made no concessions to adornment; it is marked by only the finest of pleats that taper to a V, a slightly bloused line at the front and sides and a neckline cut bolero-style at the back.

Chanel's black afternoon dresses remained equally discreet. In 1928, a few flared

Previous pages
Long ruched bodice and black chiffon skirt hemmed with fine Chantilly lace. The cape, short in front and flared in the back, recalls a pair of wings. Movement, light and airiness are the keywords. Photo Georges Saad, *L'Art et la Mode*, March 1961.

Opposite
The 'Ford' dress created in 1926, a symbol of the Chanel style. Sketch by Karl Lagerfeld.

Portrait imaginaire de Coco Chanel

dans sa robe "Ford" de 1926

Karl Lagerfeld 90

Left
Black knee-length sheath dress with a pastel pink jabot, paired with an out-of-this-world giant camellia. 2002 Spring–Summer Haute Couture. Photo Karl Lagerfeld.

Opposite
A classic black dress, with bloused bodice and long sleeves. Reconstruction by Karl Lagerfeld of a design dating from 1926. Photo Karl Lagerfeld.

Opposite
Lace dress with floating
panels of chiffon. The
deep scoop of the back
is accentuated with pearl
sautoirs. Illustration from
Vogue France, 1927.

Right
Lightness and elegance
for this evening gown in
black raised lace with a
large black tulle flounce.
Vogue France, April 1936.
Photo André Durst.

'Before me, no one would have dared to dress in black.'

flounces accentuated the 'minaret' effect of a design in Moroccan crêpe. In 1929, a yoked cape drapes elegantly over the pure lines of a tunic. Pleats and folds soften the bodice, the skirt is fuller but the spirit is the same. Mademoiselle, who had a certain taste for frivolity, advocated 'the audacity of nothing' in this already iconic dress, often made of matte crêpe, satin or satin crêpe. She used both sides of the fabric to create a tone-on-tone matte/gloss effect. Contrasting white trimmings – collars, cuffs, flowers and strings of pearls – sometimes highlighted this constant (false?) modesty. For cocktails, eveningwear or special occasions, black was

king. Though Chanel promoted the black dress for eveningwear, she continued to shun gratuitous showiness and ostentation. It was her skilled use of fabrics, layering and shine that gave soul to these remarkably modern creations.

By the late twenties, she had begun to create sheath dresses with low-cut backs, draped in featherweight chiffons, designs in tulle with plunging backs and pleated, layered flounces, and bustier dresses made entirely of lace. A 1931 model is made of black ciré crêpe de Chine topped with a black velvet jacket. In the vanguard of modernity, other models in ciré satin or encrusted with sparkling sequins were so ahead of their time that they were still being revived twenty, thirty or forty years later, adapted to suit the spirit of the day. Mademoiselle accessorized these dresses – always black, always simple – with oversized gold jewelry or pearl sautoirs. It is often said that Coco Chanel was the first great stylist. She was certainly one of the first to recognize the importance of accessories, and the little black dress gave her the opportunity to prove it with every one of her creations.

It was her genius for deceptive simplicity combined with her personal concept of chic that convinced Hollywood magnate Samuel Goldwyn to contact her in 1930. He sensed that she alone could give his stars a modern and truly Parisian look. Her talent for making black look luxurious fascinated the producer, who disapproved of his actresses'

conspicuous extravagance during the years of the Depression. The movie tycoon offered Mademoiselle an annual income to create two collections for MGM's greatest stars. What an idea: Claudette Colbert, Gloria Swanson, Greta Garbo, Marlene Dietrich wearing Chanel clothes both on and off stage! Intractable as ever and despite slight misgivings about the partnership, Coco, who was already a

'Luxury is not the opposite of poverty; it is the opposite of vulgarity.'

celebrity across the Atlantic, decided to give her image a boost. Besides, she thought Hollywood might be fun. She began by making the costumes for four films, the most famous being *Tonight or Never*, and for a Broadway play. She soon returned to rue Cambon, however. There, she didn't have to trust anyone but herself, and was free to let her own creativity and inspiration take the lead.

Her showbusiness experience did not end in America. Shortly after her return to France, her friend Jean Cocteau, with whom she had already worked, persuaded her to design costumes for his play *La Machine Infernale* (*The Infernal Machine*) followed by *Œdipe Roi* (*Oedipus Rex*). In 1938, she went on to work with Jean Renoir on *La Marseillaise* and *La Règle du Jeu* (*The Rules of the Game*), an acknowledged classic.

In the late thirties, just before disappearing into the night from which she only officially emerged in 1954, Mademoiselle determined to give women back some of their 'lost mystery'. She celebrated 'poetry in fashion', the art of creating an illusion. She even claimed, much later: 'That is one of the great joys of this profession: fashion is essential. No one can resist that illusion.'[3] The long stylized dresses in lace, tulle or chiffon, in faille or organza, sometimes adorned with sequins or special effects such as multilayered panels of chiffon or very fine panels of cellophane crafted by the ateliers are stunningly beautiful and glamorous. The house's perfectionism is apparent in the skilful combining of fabrics in typical Chanel style, transfiguring a black evening gown into a jewel in itself. Rhinestone straps, silver fastenings, lamé,

Previous pages
Black tulle and chiffon, the
quintessence of elegance.

Opposite
One of the last dresses
created by Coco Chanel
in 1939. A Grecian-style
draped gown, fit for a
dark goddess. Photo
Horst P. Horst.

Opposite

Chemise dress in black Gerondeau wool crêpe, with pleated skirt and white piqué collar and cuffs. Photo Georges Saad, *L'Art et la Mode*, 1958.

Right

The black dress in schoolgirl style with white satin collar and cuffs outlined with silver studs. Oversized studs form the sautoirs. Footless tights and shoes with ankle straps. 2003 Autumn–Winter Prêt-à-Porter Collection. Photo Karl Lagerfeld.

tulle, lace, huge satin bows, touches of gold: luxury, perfection and elegance became the hallmarks of Chanel Haute Couture.

While the fashionable elite was quick to turn the little black dress into an institution, actresses of the day were no less sensitive to the appeal of black, to the aura of mystery it created, its captivating allure, its power to seduce – the colour of an obscure object of desire. A black dress transformes a woman into a goddess. In 1931, the celebrated silent movie actress Gloria Swanson starred in *Tonight or Never* wearing a long black dress adorned with cleverly arranged straps. In 1939, Mila Parély in *La Règle du Jeu* donned a black tulle dress embroidered with camellias. The little black dress returned to the screen in 1954, in simple black velvet, light silk chiffon or fitted lace. It appealed to the period, to society women and to film stars. Jeanne Moreau, femme fatale in *Les Amants* (*The Lovers*) and *Les Liaisons Dangereuses*, was completely devoted to black. Delphine Seyrig in *L'Année Dernière à Marienbad* wore a fluid chiffon dress that was to leave its mark in fashion history and on the cinema of the sixties. By then, Chanel was being copied, plundered even, but she didn't mind. On the contrary, she fully intended to leave a legacy of sorts to her imitators – anonymous dressmakers and seamstresses – ideas that would last more than a season and outlive fashion to become a style. She wanted her creations to be imitated in the streets. She declared:

'Everybody was wearing a little black dress with a little something, movie stars, chambermaids.'

'A fashion that goes out of fashion overnight is a distraction, not a fashion.'[4] The future was to prove how right she was.

Seeing the young stars of today clad in dresses that Coco Chanel designed or could easily have designed is amazing. What better proof than the stunning long dress with layered lace flounces worn by Vanessa Paradis with such youthful grace! This 1938 creation could have been designed at the beginning of the 21st century. Whether it is an illusion or allusion to a modern classic, modern celebrities continue to wear black by night to highlight their youth and

Opposite
Photographed in Mademoiselle's apartment, a lace dress with décolleté and elbow-length sleeves. The play of subtle transparency enhances porcelain skin. Haute Couture 1957. Photo Henry Clarke.

Delphine Seyrig in a chiffon
dress with floating panels
immortalized in *Last Year at
Marienbad*, the legendary
movie by Alain Resnais.

beauty. Penelope Cruz chose a dress with a long-line boned bodice over a full and flounced skirt; Kirsten Dunst, a lace sheath; Kate Hudson, a close-fitting number with a lace inset; Sofia Coppola, sheer braided chiffon; Kylie Minogue with her beautiful porcelain skin, a black velvet version with a deep V-neck and puffed sleeves in a display of timeless luxury.

But why was Coco Chanel so fascinated by black, a fascination that lasted her whole life? What fuelled this love of darkness, silence and the night? What memories, what places left such an indelible impact on her? Her biographers provide a Freudian analysis – 'Black is her childhood, the parents she lost too young. Black symbolizes the dormitory walls of the Aubazine orphanage where her father, an itinerant market trader, abandoned her after her mother's death. Black is the symbol, the colour of death, and perhaps more so for her, the colour worn by the Limousin peasants of her youth. But above all, it is the colour of the abyss into which the death in December 1919 of Arthur Boy Capel, the great love of her youth, plunged her'.[5] 'Solitude is awkwardness,'[6] she used to say, though she never feared it. She liked to relive her memories as they streamed before her eyes, as on a catwalk. Nor was she afraid of darkness. Black was so deeply entrenched in her soul and so desirable to her that she used it in her home as a leitmotif, in touches of shiny lacquer to neutralize the gold, bronze and baroque ornaments, 18th-century armchairs, Regency tables, crystal chandeliers and Venetian mirrors.

With her jet-black hair and onyx eyes, black encapsulated the beauty of Coco Chanel. She dressed in black from the trimmings on her hat to the tips of her two-tone shoes. Chanel's black captures light and manipulates it with consummate skill, using fabric, cut, embroidery, contrasts of texture,

Opposite above
Sparkling sequins on
matte silk, a detail of a
design from the 1930s.
Chanel collection.

Right
Vanessa Paradis sporting
a bustier dress in black
embroidered tulle, designed
by Coco Chanel in 1938.
Elle, March 2004.
Photo Karl Lagerfeld.

Opposite
Cocktail dress in chiffon with pencil pleats, worn by Marie-Hélène Arnaud. Spaghetti straps, corselet and satin ribbons to emphasize the waist. Photo Peter Fink, 1959.

Right
Elegance and simplicity for this majestic sheath dress. Photo Karl Lagerfeld.

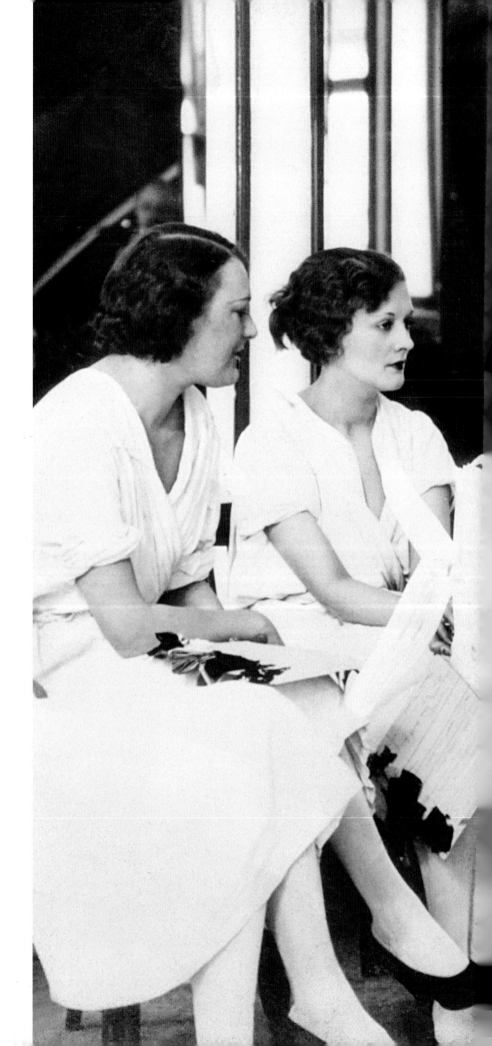

Mademoiselle attends
a fitting session with
Lady Pamela Smith and
a circle of young society
ladies. London 1932.
Photo Bettmann.

diaphanous net, chiffon, tulle and gauze, flounces, layering, accessories, and jewelry to add the lustre of pearls, scintillating gold, or the deep colours of baroque gems.

Her passion for black, that non-colour, her signature, stayed with her to the end. She even had it incorporated into her double C logo, and the little black Bakelite boxes for holding makeup and other magical products. To this day, black remains emblematic of Chanel, a prelude to the mysteries of elegance.

'I am a black diamond, still uncut. A black diamond is very rare, hard to cut, so not easy to market.'[7] The words Karl Lagerfeld used to define himself could easily be applied to the little black dress, that jewel that he 'cuts' like no one else and which is often the star piece of his collections. No folklore, no strategy, not the slightest concept of marketing, which he loathes and distrusts more than anything. For the couturier who continues Mademoiselle's painstaking work, the little black dress epitomizes the Chanel philosophy.

Ever since it was introduced, there has always been a little black dress to match the spirit of the times. There is nothing constant or basic about it. Its look, style, cut and silhouette are reinvented each season, moulded by his imagination, fantasies, creativity and passion. For the 2003 Autumn–Winter Prêt-à-Porter collection, an ultra-short version with fluid lines

recalled a schoolgirl's pinafore, worn over leather leggings. The dress returned to the catwalk in black tweed with round cut-outs covered with double-sided black satin ribbon fixed with giant pins. A witty nod to biker girls or punks, perhaps? Not really

'A black so deep, so noble that once seen, it stays in the memory forever.'

because a touch of black lace peeked out from under the dress, recalling Chanel's fundamental femininity and elegance. For the 2004 Autumn–Winter Haute Couture collection, the designer used lace and sequinned lamé for low-necked sheaths topped with a ruched chiffon shawl jacket. On other occasions, his black dresses have been a living expression of the timeless

Opposite
Black muslin dress with three-tiered top and narrow black appliqué silk ribbons. The vertically applied ribbons float freely towards the hem. 2005–2006 Autumn–Winter Prêt-à-Porter. Photo Karl Lagerfeld.

Opposite
Evening variations:
long dresses with layered
flounces or small trains.
Backstage photo by
Thibaut de Saint-Chamas.
2004 Autumn–Winter
Haute Couture.

Right
Model Marion Morehouse
in a 'mermaid' dress from
1929. Slits and a fishtail
skirt shows off the figure.
Photo Edward Steichen.

Previous pages
2004–2005 Autumn–
Winter Haute Couture.
Cocktail and evening
gowns in muslin and lace.
Photos Karl Lagerfeld.

Opposite
Daria, a languorous lady
in black velvet under the
lights of Place Vendôme.
2005 Spring–Summer
Boutique catalogue.
Photo Karl Lagerfeld.

Chanel vision, as in the playful grand finale of his 2005 Autumn–Winter Prêt-à-Porter collection. Far from considering the black dress as the sort of all-purpose ever-fashionable staple every woman should have in her wardrobe, Karl Lagerfeld has transformed it into an infinitely versatile garment, an embodiment of the spirit of the day, by turns provocative, poetic, vibrant,

'A well-tailored dress suits everyone.'

and – more and more often – sumptuous. A true fashion magician, he treats the multifaceted dress in a playful style and relies on the expertise of the haute couture ateliers. 'Haute couture enables you to do everything', he explains. 'It's the laboratory of ideas.' Even the most outrageous, the most extravagant and the most expensive of ideas are welcomed, even encouraged. Lagerfeld sees haute couture as giving rise

to new trends which are then passed on to Prêt-à-Porter. Though haute couture reflects the purest Chanel tradition, it remains a discipline that leaves little room for error but nonetheless provides moments of sheer bliss. It may be ephemeral, but it can also be utterly dazzling.

Simple black, as featured in recent couture collections: an evening dress with a skirt made of layers of entirely embroidered lace; a sheath jacket over a column skirt with a cascade of dreamy tiered embroidery. At the 2005 Autumn–Winter Haute Couture collection, the audience watched in awe as creations of breathtaking black magic streamed by; exquisite, sublime black dresses, many of which were entirely hand-embroidered by the Lesage ateliers. One dress, for instance, was a reproduction of a thirties Art Deco design and took an astonishing nine hundred hours to make! This performance was a perfect illustration of how the 'little' black dress can be transfigured by the art of sumptuous luxury.

Grande finale of the
2005 Autumn–Winter
Prêt-à-Porter Collection.
Variations on the theme
of the little black dress,
designed and styled
by Karl Lagerfeld.
Photo Fédérique Dumoulin.

BIBLIOGRAPHY & NOTES

Jean-Marie Floch, *L'Indémodable total look de Chanel*, Paris: Institut Français de la Mode, Éditions du Regard, 2004

Amy de la Haye and Shelley Tobin, *Chanel: The Couturiere at Work,* London: Victoria & Albert Museum, 1994

Paul Morand, *L'Allure de Chanel*, Paris: Hermann Editeurs des Sciences et des Arts, 1996

Patrick Mauriès, *Jewelry by Chanel*, London: Thames & Hudson, 1993

François Baudot, *Chanel, Mémoire de la Joaillerie*, Paris: Assouline, 2003

INTRODUCTION

QUOTATION
p. 9. Coco Chanel quoted by Claude Delay, *Chanel Solitaire*, Paris: Gallimard, 1983.

THE SUIT

QUOTATIONS
p. 12. Coco Chanel quoted by Paul Morand, *op. cit.*
p. 21. Coco Chanel quoted in an article by Madeleine Chapsal, *L'Express,* 11 August 1960.
p. 28. Coco Chanel quoted by Edmonde Charles-Roux, *L'irrégulière ou mon*

Itinéraire Chanel, Paris: Grasset, 1974.
p. 36. Coco Chanel quoted by Paul Morand, *op.cit.*
p. 43. Spinoza, quoted by Karl Lagerfeld in an interview with *iD Magazine*, April 2005.
p. 49. Coco Chanel quoted in an article by Yves Salgues and Geneviève Vigier, *Jours de France*, 24 February 1962.

NOTES
1. Paul Morand, *op.cit.*
2. Jules Renard, *Journal*, 19 March 1901.
3. Paul Morand, *op. cit.*
4. Claude Delay, *op. cit.* p. 9.
5. Paul Morand, *op. cit.*
6. Claude Delay, *op. cit.* p. 9.
7. Paul Morand, *op. cit.*
8. *Ibid.*
9. Jean Cocteau quoted in an article by Yves Salgues and Geneviève Vigier, *Jours de France*, 24 February 1962.
10. Karl Lagerfeld quoted in the article 'Karl le téméraire' by Serge Raffy, *Le Nouvel Observateur,* 1–7 July 2004.
11. Karl Lagerfeld, *ibid.*

THE CAMELLIA

QUOTATIONS
p. 52. Press file 'Les éléments d'identification instantanée de Chanel'
p. 56. Coco Chanel quoted by Claude Delay, *op.cit.* p. 9.
p. 63. Excerpt from 'Réflexions de Coco Chanel' published in the *Album du*

Figaro, December 1950.

p. 68. Coco Chanel quoted by Paul Morand, *op.cit.*; also in Jean Leymarie, *Chanel*, New York: Skira, 1987.

p. 75. Coco Chanel quoted by Pierre Galante, *Les Années Chanel*, Paris: Mercure de France, 1972.

NOTES

1. Roland Barthes, 'Des joyaux aux bijoux', *Jardin des Modes*, April 1961.

JEWELRY

QUOTATIONS

p. 90. Coco Chanel quoted in the article 'Le luxe de Paris contre le chômage', *L'Intransigeant*, 26 October 1932.

p. 94. Press file 'Bijoux de Diamants', 1932. This text bears Mademoiselle Chanel's signature.

p. 104. Coco Chanel quoted by Marcel Haedrich, *Coco Chanel*, Paris: Belfond, 1987, and Jean Leymarie, *Chanel, op.cit.* p. 68.

p. 109. Coco Chanel quoted by Paul Morand, *op.cit.*

p. 118. Coco Chanel quoted in *L'Intransigeant, op.cit.* p. 90.

p. 121. Coco Chanel quoted in 'Gabrielle Chanel nous parle', *L'Intransigeant*, 8 November 1952, quoted by Patrick Mauriès, *op.cit.*

NOTES

1. Press file 'Bijoux de diamants', 1932.

This text bears Mademoiselle Chanel's signature.

2. *Vogue* France, January, 1933.

3. Press file 'Bijoux de diamants', 1932

4. Interview by Albert Flamand, *L'Illustration,* 12 November, 1932.

5. *Vogue* France, January, 1933.

6. Paul Morand, *op.cit.*

7. Paul Morand, *op.cit.*

FRAGRANCE & BEAUTY

QUOTATIONS

p. 124. Coco Chanel quoted by Marcel Haedrich, *op.cit.* p. 104.

p. 129. Coco Chanel quoted by Paul Morand, *op.cit.*

p. 134. Coco Chanel quoted by Paul Morand, *op.cit.*

p. 139. 'Maximes et Sentences' by Gabrielle Chanel, *Vogue*, September 1938.

p. 140. Coco Chanel quoted by Claude Delay, *op.cit.* p. 9.

p. 153. Answer in an interview with Jacques Chazot for the TV show *Dim Dam Dom*, film by Guy Job, 1969.

p. 157. Coco Chanel quoted by Claude Delay, *op.cit.* p. 9.

NOTES

1. Colette, quoted by Edmonde Charles-Roux, *Le Temps Chanel*, Paris: Éditions de La Martinière, 2004.

2. *ibid.*

3. Paul Morand, *op.cit.*

4. *Ibid.*

5. *Ibid.*

6. *Ibid.*

7. Pierre Galante, *op cit.* p. 75

8. *Ibid.*

THE BLACK DRESS

QUOTATIONS

p. 164. Coco Chanel quoted by Paul Morand, *op.cit.*

p. 168. Coco Chanel quoted by Claude Delay, *op cit.* p. 9.

p. 175. Coco Chanel quoted by Marcel Haedrich, *op. cit.* p. 104.

p. 178. Coco Chanel quoted in *Jours de France,* 7 May 1960

p. 182. Coco Chanel quoted by Marcel Haedrich, *op. cit.* p. 104

p. 192. Coco Chanel quoted by Edmonde Charles-Roux, *op.cit.* p. 28

p. 199. Coco Chanel quoted by Paul Morand, *op.cit.*

NOTES

1. Paul Morand, *op. cit.*

2. *Ibid.*

3. Article by Yves Salgues and Geneviève Vigier, *Jours de France,* 24 February 1962.

4. *Ibid.*

5. Éric Fontaine, *Le Monde*, quoted by Paul Morand, *op.cit.*

6. Edmonde Charles-Roux*, op.cit.* p. 28.

7. 'La méthode K', article by Catherine Maliszewski, *Le Figaro,* 18 January, 2005.

PHOTO CREDITS

The collection pieces entrusted to us by Chanel for this book were photographed by Fabien Sarazin.

p. 85 Ramsay/Fabien Sarazin
p. 86 Ramsay/Fabien Sarazin
p. 87 Chanel/ Karl Lagerfeld.

JEWELRY

p. 88 Robert Bresson
p. 91 Roger Schall
pp. 92–93 Fabien Sarazin
p. 95 Ramsay/Fabien Sarazin
p. 96 Chanel Joaillerie
p. 97 Lee Jenkins
p. 98 Chanel Joaillerie
p. 99 Chanel Joaillerie
p. 100 Chanel/Karl Lagerfeld
p. 101 Chanel Joaillerie
pp. 102–103 Ramsay/Fabien Sarazin
p. 105 Ramsay/Fabien Sarazin
p. 106 Ramsay/Fabien Sarazin
p. 107 Ramsay/Fabien Sarazin
p. 108 Mission du Patrimoine
photographique, Paris
p. 110 Chanel Joaillerie
p. 111 Chanel Joaillerie
p. 112 Chanel Joaillerie
p. 113 Madame Figaro/Pascal Chevalier
p. 115 Ramsay/Fabien Sarazin
pp. 116–117 Lee Jenkins
p. 119 Lipnitzki/Viollet
p. 120 Chanel/ Patrick Demarchelier.

FRAGRANCE & BEAUTY

p. 122 Chanel/Didier Roy
p. 125 Hulton Getty

pp. 126–127 Ramsay/Fabien Sarazin
p. 128 Chanel/Karl Lagerfeld
p. 130 Ramsay/Fabien Sarazin
p. 131 Ramsay/Fabien Sarazin
p. 132 Ramsay/Fabien Sarazin
p. 133 Ramsay/Fabien Sarazin
p. 135 Unknown photographer
pp. 136–137 Ramsay/Fabien Sarazin
p. 138 Daniel Jouanneau
p. 141 Ramsay/Fabien Sarazin
pp. 142–143 Ramsay/Fabien Sarazin
p. 144 Ramsay/Fabien Sarazin
p. 145 Ramsay/Fabien Sarazin
p. 146 Ramsay/Fabien Sarazin
p. 147 Mission du Patrimoine
Photographique, Paris
pp. 148–149 Ramsay/Fabien Sarazin
p. 150 Chanel/ Karl Lagerfeld
p. 151 Chanel/Wolfgang Ludes
p. 152 Richard Avedon
pp. 154–155 Chanel 1997/Copyright
Andy Warhol Foundation
p. 156 Chanel
pp. 158–159 Catherine Deneuve
photographed by Richard Avedon
for Chanel N°5. Advertising campaign
reserved exclusively to the United States
from 1968 to 1977.
p. 161 Chanel/Sketch Karl Lagerfeld.

THE BLACK DRESS

p. 162 Chanel/Karl Lagerfeld
p. 165 Sygma
pp. 166–167 Georges Saad

p. 169 Chanel/Karl Lagerfeld
p. 172 (background) Ramsay/F. Sarazin
p. 173 Vogue Paris
p. 174 Vogue Paris
pp. 176–177 Ramsay/Fabien Sarazin
p. 179 Condé Nast Publications Ltd
p. 180 Georges Saad
p. 181 Chanel/Karl Lagerfeld
p. 183 ADAGP/Henry Clarke, 2005
p. 186 Ramsay/Fabien Sarazin
p. 187 Chanel/Karl Lagerfeld
p. 188 Peter Fink
p. 189 Chanel/Karl Lagerfeld
pp. 190–191 Corbis
p. 194 Thibaut de Saint-Chamas
p. 195 Condé Nast Archive/Corbis
p. 170 Chanel/Karl Lagerfeld
p. 171 Chanel/Karl Lagerfeld
pp. 184–185 BIFI
p. 193 Chanel/Karl Lagerfeld
p. 196 Chanel/Karl Lagerfeld
p. 197 Chanel/Karl Lagerfeld
p. 198 Chanel/Karl Lagerfeld
pp. 200–201 Chanel/Frédérique
Dumoulin/Java.

*In some cases,
despite our research efforts,
we were not able to identify
certain agencies or retrace certain
photographs. The publisher
is at the disposal of any rightful
owners wishing to make a claim.*

OUR WARMEST THANKS TO :

Odile Babin
Vanessa Bongrand
Marie-Louise de Clermont-Tonnerre
Céline Clot-Polisse
Patrick Doucet
Valérie Duport
Marika Genty
Cécile Goddet-Dirles
Jacques Helleu
Karl Lagerfeld
Julie Le Blevec
Katherine Marre
Dominique Moncourtois
Françoise Montenay
Heidi Morawetz
Émilie Motheau
Philippe Mougenot
Julie Pedegert
Véronique Pérez
Eric Pfrunder
Jacques Polge
Sophie Vergès

AND TO :
François Lesage (Paraffection embroidery atelier)
Geneviève Renault, Director of Lemarié (Paraffection atelier)